# THE GREAT BOOKS

*because women say so!*

Chosen by Readers in More Than 300
Book Ventures—Groups, Retreats, and Travels

*1986-2007*

**BookWomen Center for Feminist Reading**
**Minnesota Women's Press, Inc.**

Third Edition
ISBN 0-9712317-9-6
BookWomen Center for Feminist Reading
Minnesota Women's Press, Inc.
771 Raymond Avenue, St. Paul, MN 55114
(651) 646-3968
www.womenspress.com
books@womenspress.com

# TABLE OF CONTENTS

*Welcome to the Great Books*                          5
  *"Great" because we say so!*                         7

*Part One: The Great Books*                           11
  *Annotated, alphabetically by title*                12
  *By author*                                         65
  *By genre*                                          72
  *Book awards*                                       81
  *For children of all ages*                          82

*Part Two: Book Ventures*                             87
  *Groups*                                            88
  *Retreats*                                          92
  *Travels*                                          100

# WELCOME...

... to the world of Great Books!

Not the "great books" of the traditional canon—mostly books by dead white males—but the rich and exciting world of memorable books written by women, all kinds of women.

The Great Books list wouldn't exist without the adventurous readers who've participated in book ventures—groups, retreats and travels—conducted by Minnesota Women's Press, Inc., since 1986. Through their insights and enthusiasms, their lively discussions, and their commitment to women's words, these readers have honored the work of all the women writers they've read.

Every year we ask members of each book venture to select the book—of all the books they read for that group, retreat or book trip—that most intrigued, inspired and stretched them, that provoked strongest response and discussion, that was important to have read, and that they wanted to be sure other readers know about. In the 21 years from 1986 through 2007, more than 3,000 audacious participants in more than 300 groups have dared to immerse themselves in books by women and to name some as "great." These titles have become our Great Book List. They're great because we say so!

We take great pride in offering our 413 Great Books, as chosen by readers who have been touched by them.

Glenda Martin, Mollie Hoben and Denise Scheibe

*Expropriating the venerated "great books" title for ourselves was a bold step to take. If you're wondering how and why we came to do it, turn the page.*

# "GREAT" BECAUSE WE SAY SO!

*A brief history of the Great Books of the Western World ("Women need not apply") and the upstart Great Books list from Minnesota Women's Press, Inc., where women set the standard. By Mollie Hoben.*

Ah, the power of naming.

When Glenda Martin decided to expropriate the designation "great book" from the dead white males to whom it traditionally was awarded and apply it instead to books by women, she acted partly with tongue in cheek. But she was also totally serious.

For decades, the Great Books program had been deciding who wrote the most important books of the Western World. And—imagine!— they were all men: Aristotle, Plato, Shakespeare, Milton, Dante, DesCartes, Melville, etc., etc.

Who decided this? Who, in other words, claimed the power of naming greatness? Two men with an agenda.

When Mortimer Adler and Robert Hutchins began to work together in the mid 1940s to promote the Great Books idea, it was a perfect partnership. Both philosopher Adler and educator Hutchins were big fans of Aristotle and St. Thomas Aquinas, and both believed that absolute truths and universal values could be derived from Western classical (i.e., male) thought.

Hutchins had been pushing this idea in the curriculum at the University of Chicago, where he was president, but he believed its real impact would come through adult education.

He started off-campus reading groups, attended at first by members of Chicago's business elite. (Are we safe in assuming they probably were groups of men?) He asked Adler, a philosophy professor at the university, to run the program.

The groups caught on, new ones formed, and soon the whole thing

This article first appeared in **BookWomen: A Readers' Community for Those Who Love Women's Words**, October-November, 1996.

got too big for the university to handle. Hutchins and Adler established the Great Books Foundation, and Adler traveled endlessly across the country, speaking and setting up groups, a "Socratic traveling salesman," as one journalist described him.

With Adler's salesmanship and a post-war yearning for what Hutchins called "education for democracy," the idea caught fire. From 167 participants in 1943, it grew to 50,000 readers in 300 cities by 1948. It became something of a fad. The mayor of Chicago proclaimed Great Books Week.

In 1952, the Great Books Foundation published its own editions of the books on the Great Books list—totaling 54 volumes, 32,000 pages, 25 million words. Every word a man's.

If we want to be charitable, we can assume that Adler and Hutchins and their (all-male) panel of experts who helped select entries didn't set out consciously to exclude women. No doubt they didn't consider women writers one way or the other. It was a given, that women's writings did not count when the Big Thinkers were being considered.

This shouldn't be surprising, since the "great" writers they admired operated out of an assumption of women's lesser value.

Consider the two teachers who influenced Adler and Hutchins so deeply. Here's Aristotle, writing in his treatise on "Generation of Animals": "The female is, as it were, a deformed male. The menstrual discharge is semen, though in an impure condition, i.e., it lacks one constituent and one only, the principle of Soul."

Thomas Aquinas, for his part, proposed that, "As God is the principle of the universe, so is man, in likeness to God, the principle of the human race."

By the way, this paraphrase of Aquinas is Susan Griffin's, and I found it, along with the quote from Aristotle, in her classic and profound book, **Woman and Nature: The Roaring Inside Her** (one of the first books on the Great Books list that Minnesota Women's Press created).

In that book, Griffin traces the history of patriarchal thinking about women and nature. Interestingly, many of the patriarchs whose misogynistic thinking she analyzes are writers whom Adler and Hutchins deemed "greats." Weaving together their pronouncements, which span the millennia, Griffin shows with chilling effect how these men, and other "great" thinkers, determined these "truths": that women are close to nature, men are above nature, and men's job is to control both women and nature.

I remember the Great Books from my childhood in the '50s. My parents belonged to a group for a while in the Chicago suburb where I grew up. I was impressed by the books themselves—the softbound, important-looking editions, which came in boxed sets—and I believed that if they were called The Great Books, they must be.

When it was my parents' turn to host the group, I would listen to the discussion from my room before falling asleep. I didn't understand much of it, but I was intrigued by the idea of adults as students, actively seeking to learn together through reading and discussion.

So, while my vicarious experience with the Great Books taught me some misleading lessons about who is worthy to read—lessons I had to unlearn later in my life—I also gained a valuable sense of book groups as a good and noble undertaking.

In 1986 (this was before she liberated the term "great books,") Glenda Martin started offering book groups at Minnesota Women's Press, Inc. These groups would read only women's works, she said.

She was not at all apologetic about limiting the reading to women (or, as some skeptics saw it, ignoring men): It was a matter of beginning to right the balance.

The body of women's writings (big, and growing) was new for many readers in Minnesota Women's Press groups, and they were amazed when they discovered so many books by women that touched their hearts, stimulated their thinking, broadened their perspectives, sometimes even changed their lives. At the same time, many were angry that they had never before heard of the books and writers they were discovering.

These reactions sowed the seeds for the Minnesota Women's Press Great Books list. If academics and critics were not going to acknowledge the contributions of women writers, Glenda said, we'd have to do it ourselves!

Thus, every book group, reading retreat and book group on the road at Minnesota Women's Press adds one (or more) titles from its reading to the list. [By 1996, groups had selected 301 books by women for designation as Great, and the list keeps growing.]

Meanwhile, the original Great Books list remained unchanged for 48 years, apparently impervious to growing awareness elsewhere in society about the limitations—not to mention injustice—of looking at anything only through male academic eyes.

Finally, in 1990, the Great Books Foundation added 60 new writers to the canon. Among them were four women: Jane Austen, Willa Cather, George Eliot and Virginia Woolf. The rare great book by a woman does exist, we were told. Four of them, in fact—out of 130.

It could be worse. Not a single writer of color made it to the list. When asked why no African Americans were included, Adler told a reporter for the Nation that it was "because no black American was necessary. No black American has written a great book."

**Thus, every book group, reading retreat and book group on the road at Minnesota Women's Press adds one (or more) titles from its reading to the list. By 1996, groups had selected 301 books by women for designation as Great, and the list keeps growing.**

Well, that's settled! No doubt Adler gave similar answers about women when the first list was announced (if anyone thought to ask such a question in the '50s).

In 1990, while Adler and crew grudgingly recognized four female greats, the Great Books list at Minnesota Women's Press contained 36 titles, and that year readers added 20 more, including ones by these greats: Margaret Atwood, Anne Cameron, Rachel Carson, Riane Eisler, Audre Lorde, Gloria Naylor and Marge Piercy.

What makes a book "great"? At Minnesota Women's Press, great books are those books written by women that have most intrigued, fascinated and challenged readers, that provoked strong response and discussion among book group members.

As Glenda says, "These books are great because our readers say they're great!"

**Update: Great Books Foundation discovers a few women writers**
In recent years, the Great Books Foundation has expanded and diversified its offerings, but changes have not affected the "traditional collection" of Great Books, which continues to include no works by women among its 75 selections.

In 1997 the Foundation created a Fiftieth Anniversary reading series of both classic and modern works. Among its 89 selections are 23 by women writers. Another newer program is the Great Conversations anthologies; these offer seven women among the 45 writers selected.

# *part One:*
# THE GREAT BOOKS

Here they are: the 413 books designated by women readers at Minnesota Women's Press, Inc. as "Great Books." We have included the copyright date for each book. Sadly, we know that some of the books are out of print; others might be by the time you read this. (And—we can hope!—some that have been out of print may have come back into print.)

**Part One** gives you the entire list three separate ways: alphabetically by title, with annotations; by author; and by genre (we've created our own, of course).

Information on the major book prizes is included at the end of the listings of the Great Books.

Since the world of children's literature is also a rich source of good reading for all ages, and since we believe strongly that every adult reader should have her own collection of children's books, we have added, to conclude Part One, a list of some of the "great books" for children that we encourage adults to read and enjoy.

**Part Two** lists our retreat "themes," our travel destinations, and many of the books read in Retreats and Travels, along with thoughts, comments by participants, and some photos of the adventures!

We hope you find in this volume information, ideas and inspiration to stimulate both your personal reading and your book group activities.

*The Greatest of the Great—148 books that have been chosen by two or more groups—are marked by a ★ and are pictured where possible.*

# THE GREAT BOOKS
*Because we say so!*

**Accordion Crimes,** E. Annie Proulx (1996). Beginning in the late 1800s and ending 100 years later, Proulx's story captures the immigrant experience in 20th century America through the life of a green button accordion.

**Ada Blackjack: A True Story of Survival in the Arctic,** Jennifer Niven, (2003). A young Inuit woman joined an Arctic expedition as seamstress and was the only member to survive.

**Address Unknown,** Kathrine Kressmann Taylor, (1938). A series of fictional letters between a Jewish art dealer living in San Francisco and his former business partner who returned to Germany in 1933.

**Affinity,** Sara Waters, (1999). An isolated young upper class Victorian woman becomes enmeshed with an imprisoned spiritualist in a notorious London women's jail.

**Ahab's Wife,** Sena Jeter Naslund (1999). Una, the wife of Captain Ahab of *Moby Dick* fame, recounts her past, from being exiled from her Kentucky home as a child, through her adventures aboard a whaler where she meets her husband, to their life together controlled by his obsession.

★ **Alias Grace,** Margaret Atwood, (1996). This novel is based on an actual sensational murder and trial in 1843 in Canada. Did 16-year-old Grace Marks kill her employer or not? Giller Prize, 1996

**All Over Creation,** Ruth Ozeki, (2003). Genetic modification of potatoes in Idaho is the backdrop for the tug and pull of a range of characters.

**All Passion Spent**, Vita Sackville-West, (1931). An 88-year-old woman asserts her independence from her family.

**Allegra Maud Goldman,** Edith Konecky, (1976). Story of precocious and funny Allegra, growing up in Brooklyn from age 3 to13.

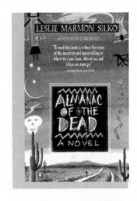

**Alma Rose,** Edith Forbes, (1993). Forbes' first novel, about a woman discovering love and her own creative spirit in a small western town.

★ **Almanac of the Dead,** Leslie Marmon Silko, (1992). A mythological, complex novel of time and land set in contemporary Tucson, AZ. With more than 60 characters, Silko presents possibility of reclaiming land by native groups.

**Always Coming Home,** Ursula K. Le Guin, (1985). A utopian vision from the life story of a woman called Stone Telling.

**American Chica: Two Worlds, One Childhood,** Marie Arana, (2002). In this memoir, Arana describes growing up in Peru and the United States. Her Peruvian father's closeknit family and her U. S. mother's independent approach to life both shape who she becomes.

**Among Women,** Louise Bernikow, (1980). A combination of literary scholarship with biography, history, politics and myth. Women talk with each other across time.

★ **Ancestral Truths,** Sara Maitland, (1993). What happened on the mountain in Zimbabwe? Clare cannot remember, even when taken home to Scotland to be with her large, loving, questioning family, where she must face the truth about her past.

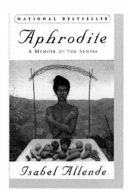

★ **Animal Dreams,** Barbara Kingsolver, (1990). A woman returning to Arizona confronts her past, finds her hometown threatened by an environmental catastrophe, and reconnects with her Native American high school friend.

★ **Annapurna: A Woman's Place,** Arlene Blum, (1980). True story of the first women's ascent of one of the world's highest peaks. This account describes both the physical and interpersonal challenges the women faced.

★ **Anything We Love Can Be Saved: A Writer's Activism,** Alice Walker, (1997). Walker continues to share her experiences and travels as she documents what she loves through poetry and essays.

★ **Aphrodite: A Memoir of the Senses,** Isabel Allende, (1998). The erotic world of aphrodisiacs, recipes, herbs and spices, as well as soups to have an orgy by, are described with humor in this visually colorful book.

**Archangel Protocol,** Lyda Morehouse (2001). In a theocracy where everyone must have an interactive computer implant, an investigator takes a case that tests her faith and courage.

★ **The Archivist,** Martha Cooley (1999). At the heart of this story are T. S. Eliot's letters to Emily Hale, and the moral and ethical dilemmas that confront the archivist who oversees them, not only in his work but also in his private life.

**The Artist's Way: A Spiritual Path to Higher Creativity,** Julia Cameron, (1992). Through a 12-week program of writing and discovery, Cameron guides individuals toward honoring creativity of self.

**Assassination Vacation,** Sarah Vowell, (2005). American history that is funny, even as seen through presidential assassinations, and how these deaths have been used for fun, profit and political advantage.

**Autobiography of a Face,** Lucy Grealy, (1994). Poet Grealy's coming-of-age story as she struggled with cancer from age 9.

**Backlash: The Undeclared War Against American Women,** Susan Faludi, (1992). With careful documentation Faludi identifies the obstacles to women's equality. National Book Critics Circle Award, 1991.

★ **Bailey's Cafe,** Gloria Naylor, (1992). A gathering at Bailey's Cafe where food is not the main ingredient but a side-dish to the magic of the human connection.

★ **Bastard Out of Carolina,** Dorothy Allison, (1992) The survival of a young girl coming of age in South Carolina surrounded by physical and emotional violence.

★ **The Bean Trees,** Barbara Kingsolver, (1988). Kingsolver's first novel introduces a heroine who "inherits" a baby, stops in Tucson when her '55 Volkswagen gives out, and becomes involved with Central American refugees.

**Bee Season,** Myla Goldberg, (2000). Eliza Naumann finds acceptance when she begins to win spelling bees, but her success rocks the foundation of her family. Her father gives most of his time to her brother, preparing him for rabbinical studies, and her mother seems involved in her law career. But the pattern is soon to change.

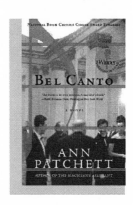

★ **Bel Canto,** Ann Patchett, (2001). A novel about the connections between human beings thrust together for a period of time. Opera and the power of music are key, as Patchett explores the humanity of jungle-born revolutionaries and sophisticated international hostages. PEN/Faulkner Award, 2002.

**The Bell Jar,** Sylvia Plath, (1971). Poet Plath's only novel is based on the events of her 20th year and her struggle with questions of living and dying.

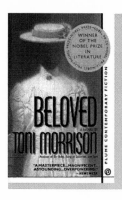

★ **Beloved,** Toni Morrison, (1987). In Ohio, after the Civil War, a mother makes heartrending choices based on her experiences as a slave. Pulitzer Prize 1988.

**Bird by Bird: Some Instructions on Writing and Life,** Anne Lamott, (1994). Witty, wise and inspiring essays for the would-be writer in us all.

**Bird Girl and the Man Who Followed the Sun: An Athabaskan Legend from Alaska,** Velma Wallis, (1997). (See **Two Old Women,** page 58.)

**Bitter Grounds,** Sandra Benitez, (1997). Set in El Salvador between 1932 and 1977, the story of passion, politics, death and love is framed by the connections of three generations of women.

**Bitter Medicine,** Sara Paretsky, (1988). In Paretsky's fourth mystery, V.I. Warshawski, a Chicago P.I., investigates a suburban for-profit hospital where inappropriate medical practice leads to the death of a 16-year-old pregnant woman from the inner city.

**Blanche on the Lam,** Barbara Neely (1992). Blanche White earns minimum wage as she cleans houses for the genteel families of North Carolina. A large, middle-aged, African-American woman, feisty Blanche has a perfect vantage point for solving murders, and she does it with style.

**Blood Shot,** Sara Paretsky (1988). Chicago private investigator V. I. Warshawski takes on big business and chemical corruption in her old South Chicago neighborhood. As in all of Paretsky's Warshawski series, social issues predominate.

**The Blue Jay's Dance,** Louise Erdrich (1996). Acclaimed novelist Erdrich writes about the birth and first months of her daughter's life, reflecting on her roles as mother, writer, woman.

★ **The Bluest Eye,** Toni Morrison, (1970). Morrison's novel of a young black girl who prays for blue eyes, believing that then she would be pretty and the family life that surrounds her would be beautiful.

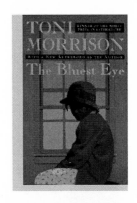

★ **The Bone People,** Keri Hulme, (1983). Hulme, a Maori, writes a complex novel of three outcasts in New Zealand, a woman artist, a young boy who does not speak and his Maori foster father. Booker Prize, 1985.

**Bones of Plenty,** Lois Phillips Hudson, (1962). Hudson depicts a proud, independent North Dakota farm family and their struggle during the Depression.

★ **The Book of Dead Birds,** Gayle Brandeis, (2003). This is a moving story of a mother-daughter relationship across cultures as each searches for her place. Winner of the second Bellwether Prize for Fiction.

**The Book of Salt,** Monique Truong, (2003). In this debut novel, Vietnamese-American Truong uses the famous literary couple Gertrude Stein and Alice B. Toklas as a backdrop for her tale of their Vietnamese chef and the reasons for his forced displacement.

**The Book Thief,** Markus Zusak, (2006). A young girl in early 1940s Germany steals books from Nazi book-burnings and from the mayor's wife's library. As she learns to read, she reads her stolen books aloud to neighbors as well as to the Jewish man hidden in her basement.

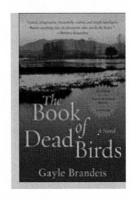

**Books and Islands in Ojibwe Country,** Louise Erdrich, (2003). Erdrich travels by boat along the Minnesota/Canadian border with her baby and the baby's father, an Ojibwe healer, teacher and spiritual leader, viewing ancient pictographs and a unique island library.

**The Bookseller of Kabul,** Asne Seierstad, (2002). Intimate description of an Afghan family, seen through the eyes of a Norwegian journalist who lived with them for several months.

**Brain Plague,** Joan Slonczewski, (2000). What if alien microbes could give us whatever our brains imagined—at a price? This futuristic biotech thriller is also a feminist and pacifist satire of human politics, a meditation on nanotechnology, artistic creativity and godhood.

★ **Breath and Shadows,** Ella Leffland (1999). In her fourth novel, Leffland moves back and forth through three generations of a Danish family, which includes a dwarf in the early 1800s, his great-granddaughter who lives near Copenhagen in the 1880s, and her granddaughter born in Illinois and living in Switzerland. A book about inheritance, roots and myth.

**Burial Ground,** Pauline Holdstock, (1991). Set in 1860 amid a smallpox epidemic, this novella tells of the culture clash between a missionary priest and a native village on the coast of British Columbia.

**Bury Me Standing: The Gypsies and Their Journey,** Isabel Fonseca, (1995). A moving and informative look at the culture and lives of a people who have been maligned for over a millennium.

★ **Cactus Thorn: A Novella,** Mary Austin, (1927). Austin's love of the southwestern desert shapes this semi-autobiographical story. Believing there is "no difference between what is social and what is personal," she weaves a tale of an eastern male politician and his connection with a self-sufficient woman of the desert.

**The Canning Season,** Polly Horvath, (2003). Two unwanted girls and a pair of eccentric old women create a quirky family, where they each find what they need in this young-adult novel that is both dark and humorous.

★ **The Cape Ann,** Faith Sullivan, (1988). The 6-year-old narrator tells of her mother's desire for a Cape Ann, a house chosen from the Sears catalogue. The story of a small Lutheran/Catholic town in Minnesota during the Depression.

**Caramelo,** Sandra Cisneros, (2002). Told through the narrator, a Chicago-born Mexican-American girl, this is the story of a grandmother who is a renowned maker of rebozos (shawls) in Mexico City, and the Chicago family who travel back and forth to visit.

**Cat's Eye,** Margaret Atwood, (1988). A Canadian woman in her 50s, exhibiting her controversial art, recalls vivid and haunting images of her girlfriends at age 10.

★ **Cellophane,** Marie Arana, (2006). An engineer and dreamer ferries his family into the Peruvian jungle. There he sets up a successful paper mill and over time masters the secret of manufacturing cellophane amid multiple human secrets and "plagues."

**The Center of Everything,** Laura Moriarty, (2003). A young girl growing up in the middle of Kansas, living with her single mother, faces the universal dilemmas of love and belief.

★ **Ceremony,** Leslie Marmon Silko, (1977). A young Native American returning from World War II finds he does not belong either on the Laguna Pueblo reservation or in the white community. To find himself he turns to the traditions of his Indian past.

★ **The Chalice and the Blade: Our History, Our Future,** Riane Eisler, (1987). Based on art, archaeology and history, Eisler tells a new story of our cultural origins.

**Chamber Music,** Doris Grumbach, (1980). A 90-year-old widow recalls her marriage to a famous American composer, her care of him in his illness, and her joyous connection to Anna, as she founds a community for aspiring artists, in tribute to her husband.

★ **The Changelings,** Jo Sinclair, (1955). Coming of age in the '50s, two young friends, one black, one Jewish, face the anger and hostilities that result from the integration of their neighborhood.

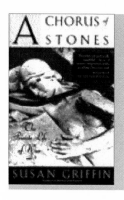

**Child of Silence,** Abigail Padgett (1993). Child-abuse investigator Bo Bradley is assigned to the case of a young boy abandoned near an Indian reservation. Her manic-depressive personality provides important discoveries as she protects the boy.

**Children of God,** Mary Doria Russell, (1998). A return mission to the planet of Rakhat, in this sequel to "The Sparrow," is centered around the consequences of the actions of the first mission. In this book, Russell further explores religious freedom, conscience, and long, skinny fingers.

**Chocolat,** Joanne Harris, (1999). Inspiration for this novel came from Harris's own background. Born in a sweetshop and being the great-granddaughter of a Frenchwoman known locally as a witch and healer, Harris uses both as a basis for "Chocolat."

★ **A Chorus of Stones: The Private Life of War,** Susan Griffin, (1992). In this book which is part autobiography and part history, Griffin writes of individual lives affected by wars, as she explores the function and meaning of war.

**Circle of Stones: Woman's Journey to Herself,** Judith Duerk, ed., (1989). A journey to the Feminine through stories, dreams and visions of women.

**A Cold Day for Murder,** Dana Stabenow (1992). This is the first book in Edgar Award-winner Stabenow's series featuring Kate Shugak, who solves murder and mayhem across Alaska.

**Cold Sassy Tree,** Olive Ann Burns, (1984). About small-town Southern life in the early 1900s, coming of age and the ties that bind families together.

**Color of Distance,** Amy Thomson (1999). Marooned in an uninhabitable rainforest populated by an amphibian species, a woman's only hope is to assimilate. This is a tale of two heroines, one human, one not.

**The Color of My Words,** Lynn Joseph, (2000). Twelve-year-old Ana Rosa Hernandez, growing up in the Dominican Republic, is passionate about writing. Through her stories she tells of the challenges her community faces and the heroism of her brother.

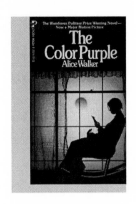

★ **The Color Purple,** Alice Walker, (1982). Novel of the difficult coming-of-age of a young woman in Georgia who finds the courage to love and to laugh after meeting her husband's female lover, a flamboyant blues singer. Pulitzer Prize 1983, National Book Award 1983.

**Companions,** Sheri Tepper, (2003). This book is set in the future when Earth is drastically overpopulated, and all resources have been depleted. On a newly discovered planet, language goes beyond words. Tepper returns to some favorite themes: ecology and animals' relationship to people.

**Confessions of Madame Psyche,** Dorothy Bryant, (1986). An orphan, growing up in San Francisco, fakes a vision of houses falling just before the great earthquake of 1906. Known as Madame Psyche, she travels to Europe and becomes a mystic.

**Copper Crown,** Lane Von Herzen, (1992). Debut novel about violent racism in rural Texas in 1913 and the friendship of two young women, one white and one black.

**The Creation of Patriarchy,** Gerda Lerner, (1986). Historian Lerner looks back at the origins of the collective dominance of women by men.

**The Crone: Woman of Age, Wisdom and Power,** Barbara Walker, (1985). An affirmation of the wisdom of older women.

**Crucial Conversations,** May Sarton, (1980). A longtime marriage ends when a wife decides to leave her husband.

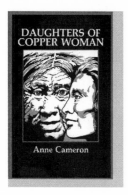

**Dance of the Dissident Daughter: A Woman's Journey from Christian Tradition to the Sacred Feminine,** Sue Monk Kidd, (1996). "I was surprised and, in fact, a little terrified when I found myself in the middle of a feminist spiritual reawakening," Kidd writes as she relates her 10-year journey to the sacred feminine. The eight pages of bibliographic notes provide the underpinnings for her journey.

**Dakota: A Spiritual Geography,** Kathleen Norris, (1993). Observations and contemplations by poet Norris, who moved from New York City back to her girlhood home in a small South Dakota town.

**Dark Nantucket Noon,** Jane Langton, (1986). One of Langton's mystery series featuring Homer Kelly. A murder takes place on Nantucket Island during an eclipse and Kelly sets out to find the culprit.

**Daughter of Earth,** Agnes Smedley, (1929). Smedley's only novel, based on her life from a poor Missouri childhood to involvement in revolutionary movements in India and China.

**Daughter of Elysium,** Joan Slonczewski, (1993). Raincloud and her husband Blackbear visit Elysium to learn of Elysians' greatest accomplishment: immortality.

**The Daughter of Time,** Josephine Tey, (1951). Inspector Alan Grant of Scotland Yard becomes fascinated with a portrait of Richard III and wonders whether he really was a villainous man of history—or was there more to the story of Richard Plantagenet?

**Daughter of the Queen of Sheba,** Jacki Lyden, (1998). A memoir by the daughter of a manic-depressive mother. A poignant story of survivors.

★ **Daughters of Copper Woman,** Anne Cameron, (1981). A retelling of Northwest coast Indian myths shared with Cameron by native women of Vancouver Island.

**Deadwood Beetle,** Mylene Dressler, (2001). As he confronts the secrets of his family's Nazi past, an entomologist emerges from his solitary professional life in New York City.

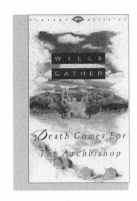

★ **Death Comes for the Archbishop,** Willa Cather (1927). A fictionalized account of the life of mid-19th century Santa Fe Archbishop Lamy, portrayed by Cather as Father Latour. Latour and his friend and fellow priest, Father Vaillant, work to win the Southwest for Catholicism.

**The Devil's Chimney,** Anne Landsman (1997). This novel explores race and gender in rural South Africa as Connie Lambrecht, dazed by alcohol and memory, becomes obsessed by 90-year-old stories of the disappearance of a young girl in a passage called the Devil's Chimney.

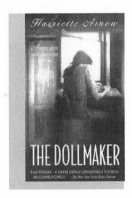

**Diary of a Zen Nun: Everyday Living,** Nan Shin, (1986). The author, struggling with ovarian cancer, finds hope through Zen as she writes of life and death.

**Different Daughters: A Book by Mothers of Lesbians,** Louise Rafkin, ed., (1987). Twenty-five mothers write about the essential questions mothers of lesbians confront.

**Different Mothers: Sons and Daughters of Lesbians Talk About Their Lives,** Louise Rafkin, ed., (1990). Children of lesbians share their stories. Lambda Award 1990.

★ **The Dollmaker,** Harriette Arnow, (1954). A Kentucky mountain woman, who creates beautiful wood carvings, is uprooted from her backwoods home when her husband moves the family to wartime Detroit to find work.

**Down the Wild River North,** Constance Helmericks, (1989). Helmericks and her teenage daughters canoe down the Peace, Slave and MacKenzie rivers.

★ **Dreaming the Dark: Magic, Sex and Politics,** Starhawk, (1982). Starhawk's message of hope for healing self, the community and even the planet.

**Dreaming of the Bones,** Deborah Crombie (1997). A literary mystery in which Scotland Yard Superintendent Duncan Kincaid is off to Cambridge at his ex-wife's request to look into a long-ago suicide.

★ **The Dress Lodger,** Sheri Holman (2001). The lives of 15-year-old prostitute, Gustine, and a surgeon who needs corpses for his medical school, are tied together in this story set in 19th-century England. Cholera is spreading through the town and Gustine turns to the surgeon to help save the life of her child.

★ **Drinking the Rain,** Alix Kates Shulman, (1995). Writer Shulman lived in solitude on a Maine island six months of every year. This is the story of what led her there and held her over the years.

★ **The Driver's Seat,** Muriel Spark, (1994). Lise is one of life's ordinary misfits, a spinster and an accountant in an anonymous city somewhere in an unnamed country in Northern Europe, who, despite the fact that she seeks acknowledgment, also seeks death.

★ **Dwellings: A Spiritual History of the Living World,** Linda Hogan (1995). Chickasaw poet and novelist explores the living world and all its inhabitants with her words on the nature of nature.

**Eccentric Neighborhoods,** Rosario Ferré, (1998). From Puerto Rico, Ferré weaves a novel, based on her mother's life, about the wealthy and the poor, of the role of women in a patriarchal society and the colonial status of the country.

**The Education of Harriet Hatfield,** May Sarton, (1989). At age 60, Harriet Hatfield opens a bookstore for women in a blue-collar neighborhood of Boston.

**The Edge of the Sea,** Rachel Carson, (1955). Carson's careful observation of sea life along the Maine coast over many years is described, in lyrical style.

**84, Charing Cross Road,** Helene Hanff, (1970). Any reader who appreciates bookstores and booksellers will find this classic memoir-in-letters to be a fascinating and rewarding read.

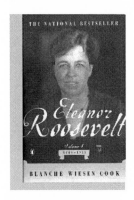

★ **Eleanor Roosevelt, Volume One: 1884-1933,** Blanche Wiesen Cook, (1992). History told around the life of a strong, dedicated woman. Lambda Award 1992.

★ **The Empress of One,** Faith Sullivan, (1996). Sullivan's fifth novel tells of Sally's growing up during the '30s and '40s in small-town Minnesota. A story of how those who differ are treated by others, some with great understanding, some with no understanding.

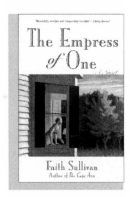

**Enemy Women,** Paulette Jiles, (2002). Accused of being a Confederate spy, an 18-year-old is imprisoned in Missouri during the Civil War. Escaping, she maneuvers across difficult territory as she returns to her home place. Each chapter begins with actual testimony from the period.

**Ethan Frome,** Edith Wharton, (1911). Tragedy blankets a stark Massachusetts farm as the three who live there find their lives spinning a web of sorrow from which there is no escape.

★ **Evidence of Things Unseen,** Marianne Wiggins, (2003). This novel describes America at the brink of the Atomic Age and the impact on a loving family's life.

★ **Ex Libris: Confessions of a Common Reader,** Anne Fadiman, (1998). Essays around the joy of words and reading by avid reader Fadiman.

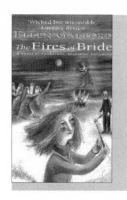

**Extra Innings: A Memoir,** Doris Grumbach, (1993). A journal of a year of writer Grumbach's life as she approached her 75th birthday.

**Face to Face: Women Writers on Faith, Mysticism, and Awakening,** Linda Hogan and Brenda Peterson eds., (2004). Essays and poems of how women envision spirit—stories with a feminine view, from multiple perspectives.

**Fall on Your Knees,** Anne-Marie MacDonald, (1996). A multi-generational tale of four sisters who live in a family steeped in secrets and lies. Set on Cape Breton Island off Nova Scotia the story begins, "They're all dead now." Secrets are revealed as the novel unfolds. Winner of the Commonwealth Writers Prize for Best First Book, 1997.

**The Family Tree,** Sheri Tepper, (1997). A book of fantasy and science fiction—funny, imaginative, mythic and archetypical. Many characters are not what they seem. Police officer Dora Henry, who is investigating the murders of three geneticists, is a great hero. However, you may never look at a weed in the same way again.

★ **The Farming of Bones,** Edwidge Danticat, (1998). This novel of a 1937 massacre on the border of Dominica and Haiti is about love, fragility, barbarity, dignity and remembrance.

**Fingersmith,** Sarah Waters, (2002). A twisting novel, narrated by two orphan girls whose lives are inextricably linked. Set in Victorian London among a family of thieves.

**The Finishing School,** Gail Godwin, (1985). A teenage girl is uprooted to a new part of the country and begins a friendship with an older woman as they explore the woods together.

★ **The Fires of Bride,** Ellen Galford, (1986). Humorous tale about a young artist who ends up on a remote island in Scotland's Outer Hebrides, where the spiritual power of women has ancient roots.

★ **The Floor of the Sky,** Pamela Carter Joern, (2006). A family saga rooted in the Nebraska Sandhills. When a pregnant 16-year-old granddaughter comes to stay with her 72-year-old grandmother, she learns family secrets and their history of connection to the land.

**For Her Own Good: 150 Years of the Experts' Advice to Women,** Barbara Ehrenreich and Deirdre English, (1978). An analysis of 150 years of disagreement between American women and "expert" professionals, especially doctors.

★ **The Forest Lover,** Susan Vreeland, (2004). Novel based on the life of fiercely independent Canadian artist Emily Carr, who painted the landscape and indigenous people of British Columbia.

**Forever Ours,** Janis Amatuzio, (2002). From her experiences as county coroner, forensic pathologist Amatuzio tells stories of love, compassion and understanding following the death of a loved one.

**Four Souls,** Louise Erdrich, (2004). This tale of revenge is vintage Erdrich.

**The Four-Fold Way: Walking the Paths of Warrior, Teacher, Healer and Visionary,** Angeles Arrien, (1993). Anthropologist Arrien presents ways to restore the balance in ourselves and in our environment.

**Frankenstein,** Mary Shelley, (1818). Written when Shelley was 19, the book dramatizes the danger of presuming to create life upon a laboratory table.

★ **The Fresco,** Sheri Tepper, (2000). When a benevolent race from another world contacts an abused Albuquerque housewife, she begins a journey of danger and redemption, for both herself and Earth.

**Frida: A Biography of Frida Kahlo,** Hayden Herrera, (1983). The tumultuous life of Mexican painter Frida Kahlo.

★ **Fried Green Tomatoes at the Whistle Stop Cafe,** Fannie Flagg, (1987). An entertaining novel of the South told in the 1980s by an elderly woman as she reminisces to her middle-age friend. Among the highlights is the story of two women who ran the Whistle Stop Cafe in rural Alabama.

★ **Fugitive Pieces,** Anne Michaels, (1996). In this lyrical and haunting tapestry of pain and healing, a young boy, whose family has been annihilated by the Nazis, is befriended by a Greek geologist. He works his way through sorrow, pain and loss to eventual self-discovery. Orange Prize 1997.

★ **Full Tilt: Ireland to India with a Bicycle,** Dervla Murphy, (1965). Memoir by one of travel writing's most adventurous women.

★ **Gate to Women's Country,** Sheri Tepper, (1988). In this futuristic country, women raise the children and shape the culture, while warrior men live in garrisons outside the town.

**Gathering Blue,** Lois Lowry, (2000). At the center is a young person who is given the responsibility of preserving the memory of the culture—and who finds the vision to transform it.

**Gaudy Night,** Dorothy Sayers, (1935). Harriet Vane returns to Oxford for a reunion and finds herself in the middle of a mystery. Who is haunting her old college? Lord Peter Whimsey comes to help and they renew their earlier attraction to each other.

★ **Geek Love,** Katherine Dunn, (1989). A novel of an unusual carnival family which includes the grandmother who ingests drugs and other noxious things to make sure her babies are special; the daughter who is hairless and humpbacked; and the granddaughter whose only uniqueness is her tail.

**Gertrude and Alice,** Diana Souhami, (1991). Gertrude Stein and Alice Toklas' friendship and love from 1907 to 1957.

★ **Gibbon's Decline and Fall,** Sheri Tepper, (1996). In the year 2000, religious fundamentalism is sweeping worldwide. A group of women, friends for 40 years, unite to defend a 15-year-old girl. Their actions affect the future of all humanity.

★ **Gift From the Sea,** Anne Morrow Lindbergh, (1955). Lindbergh's meditations on youth and age, love and marriage, solitude and contentment, using sea shells as metaphor.

**Girl with a Pearl Earring,** Tracy Chevalier, (1999). In 17th-century Holland, a coming-of-age story of a fictional 16-year-old muse who might have inspired Vermeer's painting of the Girl with a Pearl Earring.

**The Girl Within: A Groundbreaking New Approach to Female Identity,** Emily Hancock, (1989). Psychologist Hancock identifies a turning point for women between age 10 and the onset of adolescence.

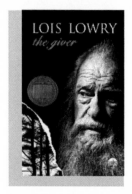

★ **The Giver,** Lois Lowry, (1993). Twelve-year-old Jonas lives in a seemingly ideal world. Not until he is given his life assignment as the Receiver of Memory does he begin to understand the dark secrets behind this fragile community. Newbery Medal winner, 1994

**The Glass Castle,** Jeannette Walls, (2005). This gritty memoir about surviving a painful childhood with parents who are loving but neglectful (to the point of abusive) raises questions about parenting, resiliency, and the tenacity of love.

★ **The God of Small Things,** Arundhati Roy, (1997). Winner of the 1997 Booker award, this first novel is of a family in southern India and the love between a man and woman of different castes.

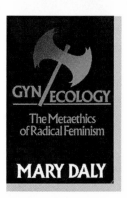

**The Goddess Celebrates: An Anthology of Women's Rituals,** Diane Stein, ed., (1991). A collection of writings on rituals by women who are reclaiming Goddess-centered spirituality.

**Going Out of Our Minds: The Metaphysics of Liberation,** Sonia Johnson, (1987). Johnson chronicles her political journeys as well as her internal transformation.

★ **Gone to Soldiers,** Marge Piercy, (1987). One of the few novels about WWII honoring the range of sacrifices and the level of support women provided during those years. The stories of six women and four men bring personal depictions of survival during dark times.

**The Great Cosmic Mother: Rediscovering the Religion of the Earth,** Monica Sjoo and Barbara Mor, (1987). The authors explore the Goddess through religious, cultural and archaelogical sources.

**Green for Danger,** Christianna Brand, (1945). A mystery set in a military hospital during a blitz in WWII. A patient dies, a nurse is murdered, six suspects surface. Inspector Cockrill investigates.

**Growing Pains,** Wanda Gág, (1940). Artist Gág's diaries from her adolescence and young womanhood.

**Guardian Angel,** Sara Paretsky, (1982). Chicago private investigator V.I. Warshawski takes on the labor unions and politicos in this 7th in a series.

★ **Gyn-Ecology: The Metaethics of Radical Feminism,** Mary Daly, (1978). Radical feminist Daly combines theology, mythology, philosophy, history and medicine as she leaps into a-mazing space.

★ **The Handmaid's Tale,** Margaret Atwood, (1985). A gripping tale, set in the near future, of women's lives when all their rights are taken away. Governor General's Award, 1986; Commonwealth Writers Prize, 1987.

**Harry Potter and the Half-Blood Prince,** J. K. Rowling, (2005). The sixth tale in the famous series is the darkest and most sophisticated yet.

★ **Hatteras Journal,** Jan DeBlieu (1987). In 1985 DeBlieu moved to Hatteras Island in North Carolina's Outer Banks. Her journal combines acute observations of the nature around her, and her reactions to it, along with scientific research and history.

**Having Our Say: The Delany Sisters' First 100 Years,** Sarah and A. Elizabeth Delany, with Amy Hill Hearth, (1993). Two centenarians recall growing up in turn-of-the-century North Carolina. This dual memoir offers a glimpse of the birth of black freedom and the rise of the black middle class.

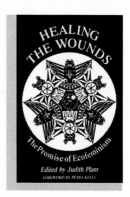

**Haweswater,** Sarah Hall, (2002). Based on actual events in the Lake District of England, this is a powerful tale of obsession, connection to the land, and the effects of progress.

**He, She and It,** Marge Piercy, (1991). Piercy explores the ethical questions raised by the creation of ever-more human-like machines as she asks the question: What makes humans human?

★ **Healing the Wounds: The Promise of Ecofeminism,** Judith Plant, ed., (1989). Essays, stories and poetry present a combined vision of feminist and ecological perspectives.

**The Heart Is a Lonely Hunter,** Carson McCullers, (1940). A young girl coming of age in a small Southern town in the '30s surrounded by a man who can't speak, a drunk radical, a disillusioned doctor and a restaurant owner. Through her connections with these lonely men, Mick Kelly searches for connection and meaning.

**Heart of the Sound,** Marybeth Holleman, (2004). How does one recover from disaster? That question is at the heart of this lyrical, elegiac response to Alaska's Valdez oil spill.

**Heir to the Glimmering World,** Cynthia Ozick, (2004). A novel of an intellectual, eccentric family escaping Hitler's Germany to an inconsequential life in the USA. A rich cast of characters ultimately pursuing the American Dream.

**High Tide in Tucson: Essays from Now or Never,** Barbara Kingsolver, (1995). Kingsolver writes of family, community and the natural world.

★ **Highwire Moon,** Susan Straight, (2001). The journeys of a Mexican migrant mother deported from the U.S. and the daughter left behind, seeking each other.

★ **The History of Love,** Nicole Krauss, (2005). Spanning a period of over 60 years, this is a story of lost love and the need to fill the void that is left.

**Holding the Line: Women in the Great Arizona Mine Strike of 1983,** Barbara Kingsolver, (1989). Kingsolver began her writing career with this book. Incorporating oral history and social cricism, the work honors the community of women during difficult circumstances.

**Holes,** Louis Sachar, (2001). For the young reader in us all, a story of Stanley, unjustly sent to a boys' detention center where every day the boys dig holes looking for something the warden is seeking. Newbery Medal, 1999

**The Home-Maker,** Dorothy Canfield, (1924). Traditional roles of husband and wife are reversed when the husband is confined in a wheelchair and his wife must work to support the family.

★ **The House at Otowi Bridge: The Story of Edith Warner and Los Alamos,** Peggy Pond Church, (1960). Part biography, part memoir, this is the story of Edith Warner, an Easterner who fell in love with New Mexico and settled there in the '30s, told by poet Church, who grew up in the remote area where Warner lived.

**The House Tibet,** Georgia Savage, (1989). Australian author writes of a young girl fleeing violence in her home, taking her autistic brother with her and joining a band of homeless children, ending up in a wondrous refuge called The House Tibet.

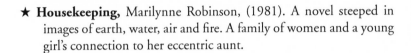

★ **Housekeeping,** Marilynne Robinson, (1981). A novel steeped in images of earth, water, air and fire. A family of women and a young girl's connection to her eccentric aunt.

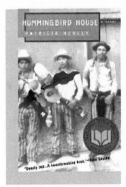

★ **Hummingbird House,** Patricia Henley (1999). Kate follows her friend to Nicaragua and Guatemala during the mid-1980s, planning to return to the United States. When her friend is killed, Kate remains in Guatemala and becomes involved with the complex political realities of the region.

★ **The Hundred Secret Senses,** Amy Tan, (1995). Olivia wants nothing to do with her half sister, Kwan, who lives in a world of Chinese spirits. But when Olivia experiences changes in her personal life, Kwan brings the pieces of their sisterhood together in a journey of faith.

**I Been In Sorrow's Kitchen and Licked Out All the Pots,** Susan Straight, (1992). A big, Gullah-speaking South Carolina woman finds meaning in her life raising her twin sons.

**I Know Why the Caged Bird Sings,** Maya Angelou, (1969). The first of five autobiographical books about Angelou's difficult early life in Stamps, Ark., and St. Louis, Mo.

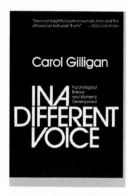

**I Loved You All,** Paula Sharp, (2000). Blending the political with the personal, Sharp creates a funny and moving novel of family life around the American politics of abortion.

**I-Mary: A Biography of Mary Austin,** Augusta Fink, (1983). Written 40 years after Austin's death, this biography provides a candid look at a remarkable, creative woman's life.

★ **In a Different Voice: Psychological Theory and Women's Development,** Carol Gilligan, (1982). Psychologist Gilligan explores women's voices and develops a female-oriented theory of moral development.

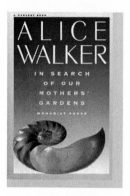

★ **In Search of Our Mother's Gardens: Womanist Prose,** Alice Walker, (1983). Essays from the '60s, '70s and '80s by poet/novelist/activist Walker, author of "The Color Purple."

**In the Company of Strangers,** Mary Meigs, (1991). Account of the making of the Canadian movie "Strangers in Good Company" by one of the women in the cast.

★ **In the Name of Salome,** Julia Alvarez, (2000). Dominican-American poet and novelist Alvarez based her novel on the lives of 19th-century poet laureate of the Dominican Republic, Salome Urena de Henriquez, and her daughter, asking, "Who are we as a people? How do we serve? Is love stronger than anything in the world?"

★ **In the Time of the Butterflies,** Julia Alvarez, (1994). This work of fiction honors the lives of four sisters who were among the leading opponents of the Trujillo dictatorship in the Dominican Republic.

**Inheritance of Loss,** Kiran Desai, (2006). From the Himalayas to New York City, the novel shows the human costs of immigration and colonialism. Man Booker Prize, 2006; National Book Critics Circle Award, 2006

**An Intimate Wilderness: Lesbian Writers on Sexuality,** Judith Barrington, ed., (1991). Essays, stories and poems of contemporary lesbian writers present a complex picture of lesbian sexuality.

★ **Into the Forest: A Novel,** Jean Hegland, (1996). Two sisters alone in the redwood forest of California learn to survive on the land as all modern systems crumble around them.

**Jane Eyre,** Charlotte Brontë, (1847). This classic novel tells the story of an unforgettable heroine, the spirited and courageous orphan Jane Eyre.

★ **Janet Frame: An Autobiography,** Janet Frame, (1982). New Zealand novelist and poet's personal struggle from poor childhood, through institutionalization, to literary recognition.

★ **Journal of a Solitude,** May Sarton, (1977). Sarton writes of her 59th year and the challenges of solitude in Nelson, New Hampshire.

★ **The Journey,** Ida Fink, (1990). Two sisters escape the Jewish ghettos of Poland and with false identity papers volunteer for work in Germany.

★ **July's People,** Nadine Gordimer (1981). A servant, July, takes a white family to his home village for safety as civil war begins in South Africa. The question of whether he is their host, their savior or their keeper is the essence of the book.

★ **Kindred,** Octavia Butler, (1979). A time-travel tale in which a contemporary African American woman is transported back to a southern plantation where her ancestors were slaves.

**Kingfishers Catch Fire,** Rumer Godden, (1953). A young English woman and her family move to colonial India, encountering heartbreak as they adjust to a different culture.

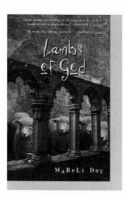

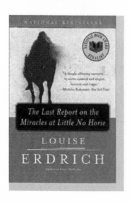

**King's English: Adventures of an Independent Bookseller,** Betsy Burton, (2005). In this history of The King's English bookshop in Salt Lake City, owner Burton writes that she has pursued a simple objective since the store's inception in 1977: "Pick good books, pass them on. That's all that counts in the end."

**Kissing the Virgin's Mouth,** Donna Gershten, (2001). A story of the strength and survival of one woman, Guadalupe Magdalena Molina Vasquez, who grows up in a poor barrio of a Mexican coastal town, experiences American affluence, and ultimately returns to her childhood home with her half-American daughter to whom she passes on her wisdom. Bellwether Prize for Fiction, 2000

**The Ladies,** Doris Grumbach, (1984). A fictionalized telling of the true story of two Irish women who eloped to Llangollen, Wales, in the 18th century and lived as a married couple.

★ **Lambs of God,** Marele Day, (1998). Three nuns, forgotten by the world, lead a quiet life on an isolated island where they tend their sheep. One day, a priest arrives, and a battle of wills and faith ensues.

★ **The Last Report on the Miracles at Little No Horse,** Louise Erdrich, (2001). The story focuses on a young priest, Father Damien Modeste, whom we meet briefly in earlier Erdrich books. His remarkable journey recapitulates the stories of some of the native peoples of North Dakota through memories, conversations, tales and reminiscences, shedding new light on these events, while his own story unwinds.

**Land of the Burnt Thigh,** Edith Eudora Kohl, (1938). Two young women homestead and become leaders in their small South Dakota community in 1907.

**The Land of Little Rain,** Mary Austin, (1903). Austin's first book is a classic of Southwestern nature literature. Ecologist, feminist, and mystic, Austin knew the desert.

**Lao Tzu Tao Te Ching: A Book About the Way and the Power of the Way,** A New English Version, Ursula K. Le Guin, (1997). Le Guin captures the poetry in English of the 81 short chapters of the 2,500-year-old Chinese spiritual classic of Tao Te Ching.

**The Last Gift of Time: Life Beyond Sixty,** Carolyn Heilbrun, (1997). A feminist shares, in essay form, her writing and reading life, as well as her life as wife, mother, academician and independent woman.

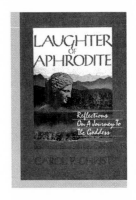

★ **Laughter of Aphrodite: Reflections on a Journey to the Goddess,** Carol Christ, (1987). Feminist theologian Christ shares her spiritual journey from Christianity to the Goddess.

**Leaving Mother Lake: A Girlhood at the Edge of the World,** Yang Erche Namu, (2003). Memoir of growing up in a remote matriarchal Himalayan culture and of the yearning to see the larger world.

★ **Letters from Yellowstone,** Diane Smith (1999). On a scientific expedition in Yellowstone Park in 1898, a young woman botanist discovers the joys of the wilderness and the passion of discovery. Winner of the Pacific Northwest Booksellers Association Award for Fiction, 1999.

**Letters to May,** Eleanor Mabel Sarton, (1986). Thirty years of letters from mother to daughter, the first written when May Sarton was 3, the last, two years before Eleanor Mabel Sarton's death.

**Life and Death in Shanghai,** Nien Cheng, (1986). Nien Cheng's chronicle of six-and-a-half years' imprisonment in Communist China during the Cultural Revolution.

**Life is Goodbye, Life is Hello: Grieving Well Through All Kinds of Loss,** Alla Bozarth Campbell, (1982). A book about change, loss and healing.

**Life's Companion: Journal Writing as a Spiritual Quest,** Christina Baldwin, (1990). A guide to journal writing as a means of expanding inner horizons.

**Like Water for Chocolate,** Laura Esquivel, (1989). Exquisitely sensuous Mexican magic.

**The Little Locksmith: A Memoir,** Katharine Butler Hathaway, (1943). This memoir of transformation and spiritual truth covers Butler's childhood years, which she spent strapped to a board to cure a back condition; her eventual purchase of a house and her marriage.

**Living in the Light: A Guide to Personal and Planetary Transformation,** Shakti Gawain, (1986). Exercises, meditations and affirmations in learning to trust your creativity.

**Long Walks, Intimate Talks,** Grace Paley and Vera Williams, (1991). Drawings, poems and prose by writer Paley and artist Williams about peace and the celebration of each day.

**The Longings of Women,** Marge Piercy, (1994). Three women—an academic, a murderer, and a homeless woman—share the same longing to be valued and loved.

**The Loony-Bin Trip,** Kate Millett, (1990). Fiercely independent, Millett struggles with her diagnosis as manic-depressive and poses challenging questions to the medical establishment.

**Looking for Lovedu: A Woman's Journey Across Africa,** Ann Jones, (2001). Jones mixes travel adventure and African history in her account of her trans-Africa journey to find the matriarchal Lovedu tribe.

★ **Lost in Translation: A Life in a New Language,** Eva Hoffman, (1989). Hoffman's memoir of her early years in Poland, her teen years in Canada and her adult years as part of New York's literary world.

★ **Love Medicine,** Louise Erdrich, (1984). Saga of two Native American families across several generations, living on a reservation and in the Red River Valley of North Dakota.

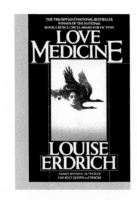

**The Lovely Bones,** Alice Sebold, (2002). This story of the ramifications of a terrible death moves from grief to hope and healing.

**Lucy Gayheart,** Willa Cather, (1935). A story of the heartache that awaits a gifted young woman who leaves her small Nebraska town to pursue a life in art.

**Luna,** Sharon Butala, (1988). In this novel of the Canadian prairie, Butala writes of farm women and the variety of life choices they made.

**Madam Secretary,** Madeleine Albright, (2003). Albright's autobiography covers her life from childhood through her time in the Clinton White House. It is very readable and a great way to read the back story on the global politics of the 1990s.

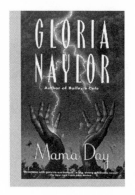

**The Magician's Assistant,** Ann Patchett, (1997). In this '90s love story the Los Angeles-born-and-bred Sabine, widow of the magician Parsifal, connects with his family on the plains of Nebraska and finds her life changed forever.

★ **Mama Day,** Gloria Naylor, (1988). Matriarch Mama Day calls up lightning storms on her Georgia sea island and struggles for her great-niece's life and soul, which are in danger from the island's dark forces.

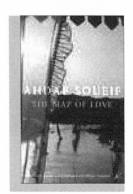

★ **The Map of Love,** Ahdaf Soueif, (1999). A novel of Egypt told through a cross-cultural love affair between a divorced American journalist and an Egyptian-American conductor, framed by the earlier courtship of the journalist's great-grandparents nearly 100 years ago.

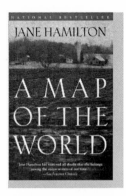

★ **A Map of the World,** Jane Hamilton, (1994). From her orchard farmhouse in Wisconsin, Hamilton writes about the precarious balance of imagined security.

★ **Maria: The Potter of San Ildefonso,** Alice Marriott, (1948). This biography/oral history tells of Maria Martinez, who became one of the most famous pueblo potters, and her people.

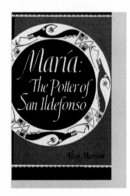

**The Master Butchers Singing Club,** Louise Erdrich, (2003). In her eighth novel Erdrich presents a tale of an immigrant German family in Argus, North Dakota, after WWI. Fidelis Waldvogel has brought sausages in his traveling case to the U.S. and becomes the butcher in this small town, where he begins an all-male singing club. A story of love, mystery, tragedy and friendship.

**Maternal Thinking: Toward a Politics of Peace,** Sara Ruddick, (1990). Ruddick explores a feminist peace politics based on the day-to-day raising of children.

**Me: A Memoir,** Brenda Ueland, (1939). Autobiography/memoir of writer Ueland's experience in Minneapolis and New York during the '20s and '30s.

★ **Mean Spirit,** Linda Hogan, (1990). Native American poet Hogan's novel of the disintegration of the Osage Indian tribe as white men take back the Oklahoma land under which oil is discovered.

★ **The Mists of Avalon,** Marion Zimmer Bradley, (1982). The King Arthur tales told from the perspectives of the women of the time.

**Monkey Beach,** Eden Robinson, (2000). Narrator Lisa Hill waits to hear word of her missing brother and recollects her turbulent upbringing in a Haisla village in British Columbia. The author is half-Haisla herself, and this is her first novel.

★ **Moon Tiger,** Penelope Lively, (1982). As 76-year-old Claudia is dying, she decides to write "The History of the World as selected by Claudia... ." She recalls her brother and daughter, and her lover, killed in war in Egypt. A complex, intricately woven novel of life, love and loss. Booker Prize winner, 1987

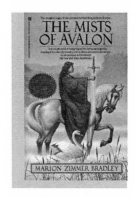

**Moonlight on the Avenue of Faith,** Gina Nahai, (1999). Nahai writes of her novel, "My hope is that whoever reads the book will see something of themselves in it." The story begins in the Jewish ghetto of Tehran and goes through the whorehouses of Turkey and the city of exiles, Los Angeles. Does Roxanna throw herself off the balcony in Tehran, or does she fly away? A book of magical realism.

**Moral Disorder,** Margaret Atwood, (2006). Eleven interwoven tales comprise this darkly witty collection of classic Atwood.

**The Mother's Songs: Images of God the Mother,** Meinrad Craighead, (1986). Craighead's paintings, with comments by the artist.

**Mrs. Dalloway,** Virginia Woolf, (1925). One day in the life of wealthy London hostess Clarissa Dalloway as she prepares for an evening party—an exploration of how the past shapes the present.

**A Muriel Rukeyser Reader,** Jan Heller Levi, ed., (1994). This collection gives a wide-ranging sampling of 45 years of Rukeyser's poetry, but as important are her far-seeing, informing connections between poetry and history, science, politics and ourselves.

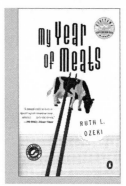

**My Antonia,** Willa Cather, (1918). Literary masterpiece about an immigrant pioneer woman on the Nebraska plains.

★ **My Year of Meats,** by Ruth Ozeki, (1998). A Japanese-American film-maker is hired by a Japanese company to film American families happy to be eating beef. As she pursues the project she discovers that the realities of the meat industry become something different than she started out to film. Kiriyama Pacific Rim Award, 1998.

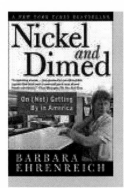

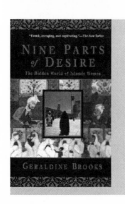

**Native Tongue,** Suzette Elgin, (1984). Linguistics professor Elgin writes of a world where all of women's rights are denied, even their language.

**The Namesake,** Jhumpa Lahiri, (2003). A tradition-bound Indian couple moves from Calcutta to Boston, where they struggle with the complexities of the immigrant experience as well as the love they have for their American-born son.

**Natives and Exotics,** Jane Allison, (2005). In this tender, lyrical novel that explores the consequences of so-called "progress," generations of an Australian family are linked across time and space by their relationships to a changing world and a common search for a true home,

**Nervous Conditions,** Tsitsi Dangarembga, (1988). Zimbabwean author presents a coming-of-age story and shows the losses involved when one culture colonizes another.

★ **Nickel and Dimed, On (Not) Getting By in America,** Barbara Ehrenreich, (2001). Reporter Ehrenreich joins the legions of working people who struggle to get by on poverty-level wages and gives us a working-eye view of what their lives are really like.

**Night Watch,** Frida Sigurdardottir, (1988). As a modern Icelandic journalist sits a death watch in her mother's hospital room, she reflects on the lives of her mother, aunt and their ancestors who lived harsh lives in rural Iceland. Nordic Council Literary Award, 1988.

★ **Nine Parts of Desire: The Hidden World of Islamic Women,** Geraldine Brooks, (1995). As a news correspondent in the Middle East, Brooks set out to learn about and understand what life was like for the women of the region.

**None to Accompany Me,** Nadine Gordimer, (1994). South African Gordimer writes of protagonist Vera Stark, a white lawyer, who represents blacks in their struggle to reclaim South African land. Gordimer received the Nobel Prize for Literature in 1991.

★ **North Spirit: Sojourns Among the Cree and Ojibway,** Paulette Jiles, (1995). Poet/journalist Jiles calls this work "creative nonfiction" in which "all the incidents are true." Jiles writes of her experience in northern Canada working on the only Ojibway-language newspaper in the world.

★ **Now in November,** Josephine Johnson, (1934). Johnson's first novel about a middle-class family driven into poverty by the Depression. Pulitzer Prize winner, 1935.

**O Caledonia,** Elspeth Barker, (1991). Depicts Scottish life through the fated main character, young Janet, a girl who finds solace in reading, learning and nature.

**O Pioneers!,** Willa Cather, (1913). Cather's first novel about the immigrants who settled the Nebraska prairie.

**Odd Girls and Twilight Lovers: A History of Lesbian Life in Twentieth-Century America,** Lillian Faderman, (1991). A scholarly study of outsider women whose sexuality and politics have affected mainstream America. Lambda Award, 1991.

**Old Books, Rare Friends: Two Literary Sleuths and Their Shared Passion,** Leona Rostenberg & Madeleine Stern, (1997). For more than 60 years these two friends shared a love of literature, becoming experts in the rare book world, and writing and editing numerous books separately and together.

**On Beauty,** Zadie Smith, (2005). Two academic rivals, differing in outlook, beliefs and family dynamics, come together in an explosive situation. Orange Prize, 2006

★ **One True Thing,** Anna Quindlen, (1994). A successful professional woman returns to her hometown, against her wishes, to care for her dying mother.

★ **Out of Time,** Paula Martinac, (1990). A stolen scrapbook of women's photographs from the 1920s leads to exploring the connections of four women who called themselves "The Gang." Lambda Award 1990.

★ **Outercourse: The Be-Dazzling Voyage,** Mary Daly, (1992). "Containing recollections from my *Logbook of a Radical Feminist Philosopher* (Be-ing an account of my time/space travels and ideas—then, again, now and how)."

**Overlay: Contemporary Art and the Art of Prehistory,** Lucy Lippard, (1983). Feminist art historian Lippard connects contemporary art to prehistoric sites and symbols.

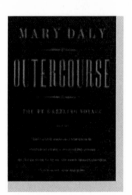

**An Owl on Every Post,** Sanora Babb, (1970). Memoir of a young girl's hard, but magical, life on the Colorado frontier in pre-World War I America.

★ **The Painted Drum,** Louise Erdrich, (2005). A rare drum found in New Hampshire, having been taken from its North Dakota Ojibwe creator, connects those who hear its sound. A story of lost children and the memories they leave behind.

**Papago Woman,** Ruth M. Underhill, (1936). A classic and readable ethnographic work, this book presents the first published life history of a Southwestern Indian woman.

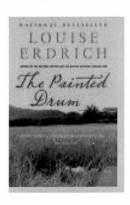

**Parable of the Sower,** Octavia Butler, (1993). In America in 2025, the gap continues to grow between the haves and have-nots. When violence alters one young woman's protected life, annihilating her family and friends, she leads a small band of followers to the promise of a new life.

**Paradise,** Toni Morrison, (1997). An all-black utopia is created in small-town Ruby, Oklahoma. But what will be done about those women living in the convent outside of town?

★ **Paris Was a Woman: Portraits from the Left Bank,** Andrea Weiss, (1995). Filled with historic photos and discussion of women-owned bookstores and independent creative women on the Left Bank in Paris from 1920 to 1940, this was a documentary film before being put into book form.

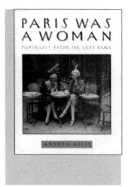

**Passionate Sisterhood: Women of the Wordsworth Circle,** Kathleen Jones, (1997). An eye-opening group biography that reads almost like a novel.

★ **Pavilion of Women,** Pearl S. Buck, (1946). On her 40th birthday, Madame Wu decides to retire from married life and find her husband a concubine. This begins her pursuit of a new way of being, enhanced by the free-thinking priest hired to teach her son English. A novel of contradictions, unorthodox Christianity, self-discipline and beauty. Buck received the Nobel Prize for Literature in 1932.

★ **Paula,** Isabel Allende, (1994). In this memoir, written as her daughter lies unconscious and terminally ill, Allende writes of her family's exile, her Chilean heritage and her love for her dying daughter.

**Persepolis: The Story of a Childhood,** Marjane Satrapi (2004). A coming-of-age view of war illustrated in a black and white graphic novel. Based on Satrapi's growing up under the Islamic Revolution in war-torn Iran.

★ **The Pickup,** Nadine Gordimer, (2001). A wealthy South African woman meets a young Arab mechanic when her car breaks down. The two seek meaning and direction in their lives. Set in the new South Africa and in an Arab village in the desert, the book illustrates a contrast between the Islamic and Western worlds. Gordimer received the Nobel Prize for Literature in 1991.

★ **Pigs in Heaven,** Barbara Kingsolver, (1989). The story of "The Bean Trees" is continued and explores the complexity of love between mother and child across cultures.

**A Place of Execution,** Val McDermid, (2000). This highly acclaimed psychological thriller by one of Britain's best-known crime writers is set in an isolated English village in the 1960s.

★ **A Place Where the Sea Remembers,** Sandra Benítez, (1993). A first novel of love and anger, hope and tragedy, in a Mexican seacoast village.

★ **The Poisonwood Bible,** Barbara Kingsolver, (1998). A Baptist missionary takes his wife and four daughters to the Belgian Congo in 1959, where war is brewing. The mother and daughters write of their lives and the different ways they are marked by the father's intractable mission and by Africa itself.

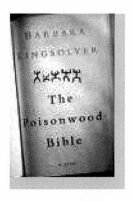

**Pornography and Silence: Culture's Revolt Against Nature,** Susan Griffin, (1981). Griffin argues that "pornography is an expression not of human erotic feeling and desire, and not of a love of the life of the body, but of a fear of bodily knowledge, and a desire to silence eros."

★ **Possessing the Secret of Joy,** Alice Walker, (1992). In this novel about female genital mutilation, the main character uses her anger to deduce meaning and understanding from the procedure she endured.

★ **Possession: A Romance,** A.S. Byatt, (1990). A novel of mystery and love as two young scholars research the lives of two Victorian poets. Booker Prize, 1990.

**Potiki,** Patricia Grace (1995). A Maori community in New Zealand tries to live the old ways and must stand up to developers who want its land. Award-winning novel by one of New Zealand's most decorated writers.

**Prism of the Night: A Biography of Anne Rice,** Katherine Ramsland, (1991). A companion work for the serious Anne Rice reader.

★ **Prodigal Summer,** Barbara Kingsolver (2000). Three intertwining stories tell of the need to protect and preserve nature and all living things.

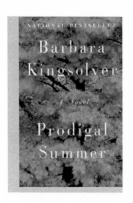

**Property,** Valerie Martin, (2003). Taking place on a sugar plantation north of New Orleans in the 1830s, the story uses the plantation owner's wife's voice to reveal the clash of wills between herself, her husband and her personal slave. Orange Prize, 2003

★ **The Prowler,** Kristiana Gunnars, (2000). This lyrical post-modern novel explores the isolation and heartbreak of a girl growing up in Iceland in the post-war years, and her later experiences as an immigrant in North America.

**Pure Lust: Elemental Feminist Philosophy,** Mary Daly, (1984). Feminist philosopher Daly explores and analyzes a double-sided meaning of lust.

★ **Purple Hibiscus,** Chimamanda Ngozi Adichie, (2003). Nigerian Adichie's first novel explores the coming-of-age of Kambili, who struggles with questions of new and old religion and with love for her wealthy father who gives to the community while terrorizing his own family.

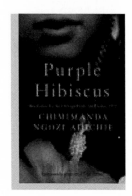

**Push,** Sapphire, (1996). At 16, Precious is illiterate, constantly abused, and pregnant with a second child. This story tells how she learns to write about her life and claim it for herself.

**Rachel Calof's Story: Jewish Homesteader on the Northern Plains,** Rachel Calof, (1995). Recently discovered memoir of a Russian Jewish immigrant's harsh life on the North Dakota prairie at the turn of the century.

**Rachel Carson: Witness for Nature,** Linda Lear, (1997). An almost 500-page biography, including 120 pages of notes, of writer/scientist Carson, who challenged how we care for the planet we live on.

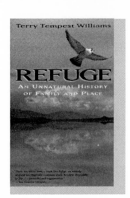

**Raising the Stones,** Sheri Tepper, (1990). Tepper's novel looks into the future and predicts humanity will survive.

**Raven's Exile: A Season on the Green River,** Ellen Meloy, (2003). Meloy and her river-ranger husband raft Utah's Green River through the 84-mile gorge at Desolation Canyon.

**The Real Minerva,** Mary Sharratt, (2004). In Minerva, Minn., 1923, three women are forced to make choices as each struggles to pursue her dreams in a society where restraints outweigh liberties.

★ **Red: Passion and Patience in the Desert,** Terry Tempest Williams, (2001). Essays and poetry of the importance of protecting the wild. Williams' dedication is "For The Coyote Clan and America's Redrock Wilderness."

★ **Red Azalea,** Anchee Min, (1994). In this true-life tale of growing up in China during the Cultural Revolution, facing constant scrutiny, Min reveals how even the government cannot squelch love and life.

**Red China Blues: My Long March from Mao to Now,** Jan Wong, (1996), Journalist Wong, a Canadian of Chinese descent, who believed in Mao when she enrolled in Beijing University in 1972, writes of her understanding of the changes in China as well as herself during the past 30 years.

**The Red Tent,** Anita Diamant (1997). From one sentence in the Bible about Dinah, Diamant creates a story to show what might have happened, and how women lived in Old Testament times.

★ **Refuge: An Unnatural History of Family and Place,** Terry Tempest Williams, (1991). Poet and naturalist Williams weaves reflections about the acts of nature and the dying of her mother.

**Re-Inventing Eve: Modern Woman in Search of Herself,** Kim Chernin, (1988). When Eve is seen as a heroine of "disobedience," her story becomes a transformative vision of woman's place in nature.

**Revelations: Diaries of Women,** Mary Jane Moffat and Charlotte Painter, eds., (1974). Selections from 32 women's diaries on love, work and power across the centuries.

**Revolution From Within: A Book of Self-Esteem,** Gloria Steinem, (1992). At the end of her fifth decade, Steinem writes, "It's never too late for a happy childhood."

**Rift,** Lisa Cody, (1988). Africa's Rift Valley was irresistible, but traveler Fay begins to realize she may never get out.

★ **Riverwalking: Reflections on Moving Water,** Kathleen Dean Moore (1995). In these essays, Moore describes her encounters with the world of rivers and in the process explores philosophical questions about motherhood, happiness, love and loss.

★ **The Road From Coorain,** Jill Ker Conway, (1989). The first female president of Smith College writes of her girlhood in the Australian outback.

★ **The Robber Bride,** Margaret Atwood, (1993). Three women, part of each others' lives since the 1960s, are traumatized when three decades later a fourth woman re-enters their lives.

**A Romantic Education,** Patricia Hampl, (1981). Author's coming of age in Minnesota and her journey to Prague as she explores her family's past.

**A Room of One's Own,** Virginia Woolf, (1929). Woolf's classic essay, which insists that a woman must have her own money and privacy.

**Roseanne: My Life as a Woman,** Roseanne Barr, (1989). Roseanne Barr's memoir, from growing up as a Jewish outsider in Salt Lake City through the creation of her TV series.

**Sacred Pleasure,** Riane Eisler, (1995). Eisler expands her partnership model to envision a society where pleasure, not pain, is the central theme of our lives.

★ **The Samurai's Garden,** Gail Tsukiyama, (1994). The Japanese invasion of China in 1930 is the backdrop for this gentle story of a young 20-year-old Chinese painter who is sent to his grandfather's house in Japan to regain his health.

**The Scalpel and the Silver Bear: The First Navajo Woman Surgeon Combines Western Medicine and Traditional Healing,** Lori Alvord and Elizabeth Cohen Van Pelt, (1999). In this memoir, Alvord describes her education in culture, first as a Navajo medical student at Dartmouth and Stanford, then as a Western-trained surgeon treating Indian patients. She emerges with a holistic view of healing.

**The Sea, The Sea,** Iris Murdoch, (1978). An aging theater director searchs for simplicity and solitude in a lonely house by the North Sea. Booker Prize, 1978.

**The Search for Signs of Intelligent Life in the Universe,** Jane Wagner, (1986). A hit one-woman play written for Lily Tomlin focuses on the female experience in society.

**The Secret Garden,** Frances Hodgson Burnett, (1911). Orphaned Mary Lennox is sent to a desolate English mansion where she discovers friendship, love and a hidden garden.

**Selected Poems: 1965-1975,** Margaret Atwood, (1987). One of the many poetry books of Canadian author Margaret Atwood.

**Shape of Red: Insider-Outsider Reflections,** Ruth Hubbard and Margaret Randall, (1988). Correspondence between two politically and socially active women who offer radical insights with hopeful vision.

**She Walks These Hills,** Sharyn McCrumb (1994). Mystery writer and folklorist McCrumb combines the present and past with a 200-year-old ghost story in the Appalachian mountains.

★ **The Ship that Sailed into the Living Room: Sex and Intimacy Reconsidered,** Sonia Johnson, (1991). Johnson challenges the meaning of relationships.

**The Shipping News,** E. Annie Proulx, (1993). Story of a third-rate newspaperman who retreats to his ancestral home on the Newfoundland coast. National Book Award, 1993; Pulitzer Prize, 1994.

**Shooting the Boh: A Woman's Voyage Down the Wildest River in Borneo,** Tracy Johnston, (1992). On the way to the uncharted Boh River, the author's luggage gets lost, and her circumstances go downhill from there. An engaging travel memoir of one woman's journey through the tangles of rainforest and menopause.

**The Short History of a Prince,** Jane Hamilton, (1998). A family story set in Wisconsin centered around a young boy's desire to dance and the challenges he faces growing up as he realizes he is gay.

★ **Silences,** Tillie Olsen, (1965). Olsen explores the social forces that silence the voices of female artists.

**Silent Spring,** Rachel Carson, (1962). With this book Carson altered the course of history through her concern for the future of the planet.

**The Silver DeSoto,** Patty Lou Floyd, (1987). Coming-of-age story during the Dust Bowl years in Oklahoma.

**Simone de Beauvoir: A Biography,** Deirdre Bair, (1990). Based on five years of interviews with the French philosopher, essayist and novelist.

**Singer From the Sea,** Sheri Tepper (1999). Set in the future on a planet called Haven where the inhabitants all are female, the novel poses questions about technology, religion, treason and love.

**Sister Light, Sister Dark,** Jane Yolen, (1988). A coming-of-age story based on folklore but set in the future.

**Sister Outsider: Essays & Speeches,** Audre Lorde, (1984). From her black lesbian feminist perspective, Lorde expands and enriches our understanding of what feminism can be.

**The Skeptical Feminist: Discovering the Virgin, Mother, Crone,** Barbara Walker, (1987). Walker's spiritual autobiography follows her journey away from Christianity to the three aspects of the Goddess—Virgin, Mother and Crone.

**Skywater,** Melinda Worth Popham, (1990). For 39 years the Ryders have lived peacefully in the remote Sonora desert, sharing land with the coyotes. The groundwater becomes poisoned by mine tailings, forcing humans and animals to find new places.

★ **Small Island,** Andrea Levy, (2004). Set in London in 1948, the novel tells the stories of two families, one English and one recently arrived from Jamaica, whose lives intersect and are shaped by war. Orange Prize, 2004; Whitbread Award, 2005.

**Small Wonder,** Barbara Kingsolver, (2002). Essays that explore hope and peace, written in response to September 11.

★ **Snow Flower and the Secret Fan**, Lisa See, (2005). This novel describes footbinding in China while honoring ancient secret writing, *nu shu*, celebrating friendships between women.

★ **Solar Storms,** Linda Hogan, (1995). A troubled young woman returns to her roots in the Boundary Waters between Canada and Minnesota, to learn her history and heal herself.

**The Song and the Truth,** Helga Ruebsamen, (1997). Lyrical and mysterious tale of a child's paradise lost, set in Java and the Netherlands as World War II encroaches.

**The Song of the Lark,** Willa Cather, (1915). Considered Cather's most autobiographical novel, "Song" tells of Thea Kronborg's struggle to find her artistic place. As Thea becomes a famous opera singer, she learns that the expected social role for women and the reality of the artistic life are quite different.

**Songs to an African Sunset: A Zimbabwean Story,** Sekai Nzenza-Shand, (1997). Stories and reflections of the author's return to her home village in Zimbabwe.

★ **The Space Between Us,** Thrity Umrigar, (2007). In modern Bombay, the longtime connection, as well as class divide, between a wealthy woman and her housekeeper is a tale of tragedy and hope.

**The Speed of Dark,** Elizabeth Moon, (2003). Autism is well-rewarded in the 21st-century American business world, until someone decides it is a liability requiring a new procedure to "cure" the condition.

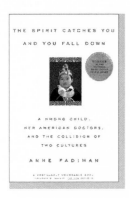

**Spending: A Utopian Divertimento,** Mary Gordon, (1998). As a woman artist turns 50, a whole new world opens for her when a man becomes her muse.

★ **The Spirit Catches You and You Fall Down,** Anne Fadiman, (1997). True story of a Hmong child, her American doctors, and the collision of two cultures. National Book Critics Circle, 1997.

★ **Spoonhandle,** Ruth Moore, (1946). A bestseller when first published, this novel tells about the Stilwell family, inhabitants of a Maine island, in whom the struggle between love and meanness of spirit, between human dignity and greed is clearly drawn.

**The Stone Angel,** Margaret Laurence, (1964). Canadian Laurence's novel creates a proud, energetic woman who struggles to hold on to self.

**The Stone Diaries,** Carol Shields, (1993). Shields chronicles the life of a woman from her birth in 1905 to her death in the mid-'80s. A novel of a woman in search of herself. Pulitzer Prize 1995.

**Stones From the River,** Ursula Hegi, (1994). Story set in a small town in Germany between 1915 and 1949, told through the eyes of a woman who is a "zwerg"—a dwarf.

**The Stories We Hold Secret: Tales of Women's Spiritual Development,** Carol Bruchac, Linda Hogan and Judith McDaniels, eds., (1986). The sacred and hidden stories of 31 women attempting to name experiences with different words.

**The Story of an African Farm,** Olive Schreiner, (1883). This classic story from South Africa presents a forthright feminist character, noteworthy for the time.

**Strength to Your Sword Arm: Selected Writings,** Brenda Ueland, (1993). A collection of articles from the Minneapolis author's last four decades.

★ **Sula,** Toni Morrison, (1973). This novel traces the lives of two black women growing up together in Ohio, one choosing to stay and one escaping; both suffering as a result of their choices.

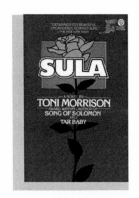

**Suite Française,** Irene Nemirovsky, (2007). Six decades after the author's death at Auschwitz, this first two of a planned five-novel cycle was discovered and published, depicting the lives of people in France in 1940-41 during German occupation.

**Summer People,** Marge Piercy, (1989). A 10-year ménage à trois changes one summer because of the presence of the "summer people."

**Surfacing,** Margaret Atwood, (1972). A talented artist, with three companions, journeys to the island where she grew up. While there, the unnamed narrator finds an inner strength to go on with her life.

**Surpassing the Love of Men: Romantic Friendship and Love Between Women From the Renaissance to the Present,** Lillian Faderman, (1981). Scholarly exploration of the cultural history of women's passionate friendships.

**Swimming in the Congo,** Margaret Meyers, (1995). Seven-year-old Grace, daughter of missionaries, comes of age in an African landscape, surrounded by both indigenous and foreign people who populate it.

★ **Tales of Burning Love,** Louise Erdrich, (1996). Set in North Dakota, this story intertwines the lives of characters from Erdrich's earlier novels. Four of Jack Mauser's five wives are trapped in a car in a blizzard and recall what it was like to be a wife of Jack.

**Tales of a Female Nomad: Living at Large in the World,** Rita Golden Gelman, (2001). For 16 years Gelman has lived "on the road" around the world; this is the story of her nomadic life, the people she has met and the cultures she has sampled.

**Talking to High Monks in the Snow: An Asian-American Odyssey,** Lydia Minatoya, (1992). Minatoya's memoir of growing up bicultural and her search from her New England roots to her Japanese heritage.

**Teaching a Stone To Talk: Expeditions and Encounters,** Annie Dillard, (1982). A collection of meditations honoring the natural world.

★ **The Telling,** Ursula K. Le Guin, (2000). Humanist science fiction from one of the best, this is a tale of spiritual quest and the cost of destroying traditional cultures.

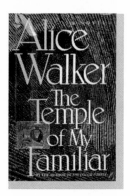

★ **The Temple of My Familiar,** Alice Walker, (1989). A tapestry of tales of dispossessed and displaced people.

**Their Eyes Were Watching God,** Zora Neale Hurston (1937). This second novel—reprinted in 1978 after heroic efforts by Alice Walker—is the most acclaimed book by folklorist, novelist and anthropologist Hurston. Protagonist Janie, whose love for Tea Cake changes her life, tells her friend Phoeby, "Two things everybody's got to do fuh theyselves. They got tuh go tuh God, and they got tuh find out about livin' fuh theyselves."

★ **These Is My Words: The Diary of Sarah Agnes Prine 1881-1901, Arizona Territories: A Novel,** Nancy Turner, (1998). Turner's novel about a woman's life in southern Arizona in the late 1800s was based on bits of her own family background. Historically and geographically accurate, it celebrates the strength of women in settling the West.

★ **36 Views of Mount Fuji: On Finding Myself in Japan,** Cathy Davidson, (1993). American Davidson teaches at a women's university in Japan. Images of Japanese culture and identity.

**Three Junes,** Julia Glass, (2002). Love between a husband and wife, between lovers, between people and animals, between parents and children is told during three separate Junes in Scotland and Long Island.

**Three Times Table,** Sara Maitland, (1990). Three generations of women, the grandmother a paleontologist, the daughter a gardener and once-promising mathematician, the granddaughter just leaving childhood.

★ **A Thousand Acres,** Jane Smiley, (1991). Modern King Lear story, told through the eyes of three sisters, as a father gives up ownership of his thousand acres of Iowa farmland. Pulitzer Prize, 1992.

**Through the Burning Steppe: A Memoir of Wartime Russia, 1942-1943,** Elena Kohzina (2001). Lyrical and moving memoir of a family's escape from besieged Leningrad to life as city strangers in a Cossack village. A daughter's tribute to her mother.

★ **The Time Traveler's Wife,** Audrey Niffenegger, (2003). The novel combines genetically induced time travel with the love story of an artist and her librarian husband.

**To Be Real: Telling the Truth and Changing the Face of Feminism,** edited by Rebecca Walker, (1995). Anthology of essays by young feminists who explore different perspectives regarding the objectives and philosophy of contemporary (Third Wave) feminist theory.

**Transforming a Rape Culture,** Emilie Buchwald, Pamela Fletcher and Martha Roth, eds., (1993). Writings by women and men about a possible future without rape.

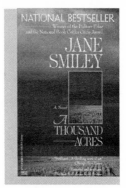

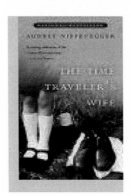

**The Travelling Hornplayer,** Barbara Trapido (2000). In a bleak twist of fate, the accidental death of a teenage schoolgirl brings together a group of people in London, Cambridge and Edinburgh whose lives intertwine with tragic results.

★ **Triangle,** Katharine Weber, (2004). The 1911 Triangle Shirtwaist Factory fire killed 146 workers, most of them women, and spurred efforts to reform working conditions in sweatshops. In Esther Gottesfeld, the last remaining survivor of the Triangle fire, Weber creates a believable and memorable witness of that day.

**Truth and Beauty,** Ann Patchett, (2004). A tough, loving and heartbreaking tribute to Ann Patchett's friendship with poet and writer Lucy Grealy.

★ **Two Old Women: An Alaska Legend of Betrayal, Courage and Survival,** Velma Wallis, (1993), and **Bird Girl and the Man Who Followed the Sun: An Athabascan Legend from Alaska,** Velma Wallis, (1997). Two retellings of ancient legends by Native writer Wallis. Both feature female heroes who face great odds and must find ways to balance their hard-won sense of independence with the traditions of community.

**Under the Beetle's Cellar,** Mary Willis Walker (1995). Texas journalist Molly Cates is faced with the toughest of assignments as she covers a story of a missing school bus filled with young children.

**Unholy Alliances: New Fiction by Women,** Louise Rafkin, ed., (1988). Stories from the '80s about relationships just a bit off center.

**An Unknown Woman: A Journey to Self Discovery,** Alice Koller, (1982). Koller's solitary inward journey during a three-month retreat on Nantucket.

★ **Unravelling,** Elizabeth Graver, (1999). In 19th-century New England, a young headstrong woman goes off to work in the textile mills, leading to a decades-long rift between herself and her mother. A beautifully written tale of love and loss.

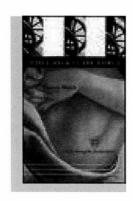

★ **Uses of the Erotic: The Erotic as Power,** Audre Lorde, (1978). An affirmation of the importance of claiming one's sense of the erotic as the source of individual power.

**Virginia Woolf,** Hermione Lee, (1999). This 800-page biography chronicles Woolf's life and the time in which she lived.

★ **Waist-High in the World: A Life Among the Nondisabled,** Nancy Mairs, (1996). Mairs' view of the world from her wheelchair, due to multiple sclerosis, challenges the negative perceptions often held by others. Both intellectual and spiritual, her memoir is told with a direct, honest and witty voice.

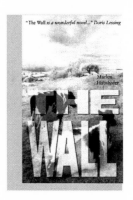

★ **The Wall,** Marlen Haushofer, translated by Shaun Whiteside, (1962). The day-by-day survival of a woman who seems to be the only survivor left on earth.

**The Wave in the Mind: Talks and Essays on the Writer, the Reader, and the Imagination,** Ursula K. Le Guin, (2004). A collection of essays grounded in the here and now.

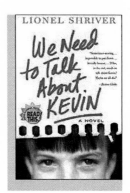

★ **We Need to Talk About Kevin,** Lionel Shriver, (2003). Through a series of letters to her husband, Eva seek to understand their raising of this son who killed seven people in his high school. Orange Prize, 2003.

**A Weave of Women,** E.M. Broner, (1978). A poetic novel weaving together a community of women in the old city of Jerusalem.

**Weaving the Visions: Patterns in Feminist Spirituality,** Judith Plaskow and Carol Christ, eds., (1989). Contributors, including Asian American, Native American and African American women, present a wide range of views about feminist spirituality.

★ **The Wedding,** Dorothy West, (1995). West, active in the Harlem Renaissance, based her novel on the life she has lived on Martha's Vineyard. She writes of the pain and joy of five generations of a black upper-class American family.

**The Well,** Elizabeth Jolley, (1986). Set in the Australian farmlands, a novel of the connection between two women, one a lonely older woman, the other a young orphan.

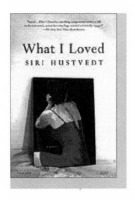

**West with the Night,** Beryl Markham, (1942). Memoir of an adventurous, independent woman who was raised in colonial Africa in the early part of the century, and became a horse trainer and record-setting aviator.

★ **What I Loved,** Siri Hustvedt, (2003). A portrait of the friendship between two men in New York City; one an artist, the other an art critic. A novel of ideas rich with the complexity of life's ambiguities.

**What Is Found There: Notebooks in Poetry and Politics,** Adrienne Rich, (1993). Rich begins, "This book is about desire and daily life."

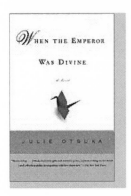

★ **When the Emperor Was Divine,** Julie Otsuka, (2002). Story of a Japanese-American family sent to internment camps in the United States during WWII. Written in spare, haunting language, this slim novel is a powerful reminder of how those who are seen as "other" are treated when a country lives in fear.

**Where No Gods Came,** Sheila O'Connor, (2003). Set in Minneapolis, this coming-of-age story explores family, love, loss and redemption.

**White Oleander,** Janet Fitch (1999). As a young 12-year-old girl grows up moving from foster home to foster home, she is haunted by the letters her mother writes from jail.

★ **White Teeth,** Zadie Smith, (2000). Smith's first novel tells the story of two families, from Bangladesh and Jamaica, who have become part of the melting pot in England. A funny book playing with ideas and language and the tragicomedy of life. Whitbread First Novel Award, 2000.

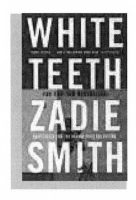

★ **Wild Swans: Three Daughters of China,** Jung Chang, (1991). The engrossing story of three generations of Chinese women whose lives spanned feudalism, revolution and cultural revolution (1909-1978).

**Wildfire: Igniting the She/Volution,** Sonia Johnson, (1989). Johnson presents a feminist anarchy, a woman-created world.

**Winter in Taos,** Mabel Dodge Luhan, (1935). A simple telling of the daily activities of Mabel Dodge Luhan in her Big House, in the Pueblo and in the village of Taos, New Mexico.

**Winter Roads, Summer Fields,** Marjorie Dorner, (1992). A collection of stories of families in a Midwestern farm community.

**Wisdom of the Heart: Working With Women's Dreams,** Karen Signell, (1990). A journey into the world of the female unconscious, based on a feminist perspective.

**The Wise Wound: Myths, Realities and Meanings of Menstruation,** Penelope Shuttle and Peter Redgrove, (1990). A positive take on a common experience of being woman.

★ **Woman and Nature: The Roaring Inside Her,** Susan Griffin, (1978). Through science, history and imagination, Griffin presents a positive connection between woman and nature.

★ **Woman on the Edge of Time,** Marge Piercy, (1976). A Chicana woman unjustly committed to a mental institution is tuned into the future and heroically helps create a better world.

★ **Woman Warrior: Memoirs of a Girlhood Among Ghosts,** Maxine Hong Kingston, (1975). An account of growing up female and Chinese American in California.

**The Woman Who Watches Over the World: A Native Memoir,** Linda Hogan, (2001). Oklahoma Chickasaw poet and novelist writes of her personal journey of illness and healing, and of her tribal history. As an environmentalist, she honors the natural world as essential to her life.

**Womanspirit Rising: A Feminist Reader in Religion,** Carol Christ, (1979). Introduction to feminist interpretations of religion from 20 women writers.

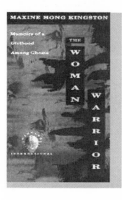

**Women and Wilderness,** Anne LaBastille, (1980). Wildlife ecologist LaBastille provides a history of frontier women as well as 15 case studies of women who currently live in the wilderness.

**Women of the Silk,** Gail Tsukiyama, (1991). A coming-of-age story in China, set in the 1920s and '30s. Working in the silk factory with other women allows Pei to find strength and independence as the women strike for freedom.

**Women, Passion and Celibacy,** Sally Cline, (1993). British feminist writer Cline writes of women who have found, in their passion for celibacy, freedom and autonomy to redefine their sexuality.

★ **Women Who Run With the Wolves: Myths and Stories of the Wild Woman Archetype,** Clarissa Pinkola Estés, (1992). Jungian analyst and poet writes about old myths from a new perspective, based on her Latina and Hungarian tradition.

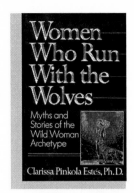

★ **Women's Reality: An Emerging Female System in the White Male Society,** Anne Wilson Schaef, (1981). A book that will let you know you're not sick, bad, crazy or stupid.

★ **Writing a Woman's Life,** Carolyn Heilbrun, (1988). Heilbrun urges women to write of their lives, to name the reality of being woman.

**Written on the Body,** Jeanette Winterson, (1992). In this novel, Winterson presents a narrator who has neither name nor gender. Lambda Award, 1993.

**Year of Wonders,** Geraldine Brooks, (2001). Based on an actual plague in 17th-century England, the novel recreates a year in the lives of the villagers who decide to seal themselves off in order to contain the disease.

**The Yellow Wallpaper,** Charlotte Perkins Gilman, (1892). A story of a mental breakdown, based on Gilman's own life.

**Yellow Woman and a Beauty of the Spirit: Essays on Native American Life Today,** Leslie Marmon Silko, (1996). From her Laguna Pueblo-Anglo heritage, Silko writes of Native American lore, religion, culture and history.

**You Just Don't Understand: Women and Men in Conversation,** Deborah Tannen, (1990). Linguistics professor Tannen writes of the complexities of communication between men and women.

★ **Zami: A New Spelling of My Name,** Audre Lorde, (1982). Lorde's "biomythography" of her childhood in Harlem and coming of age in the late '50s.

# By Author

*The list of authors contains 315 different writers whose books have been designated "Great." Forty-two are represented by mooore than one title, with 10 having four or more books on the list: Margaret Atwood, Willa Cather, Louise Erdrich, Linda Hogan, Barbara Kingsolver, Ursula K. Le Guin, Toni Morrison, Marge Piercy, Sheri Tepper and Alice Walker.*

**Adichie, Chimamanda Ngozi.** Purple Hibiscus

**Albright, Madeleine.** Madam Secretary

**Allende, Isabel.** Aphrodite: A Memoir of the Senses

**Allende, Isabel.** Paula

**Allison, Dorothy.** Bastard Out of Carolina

**Allison, Jane.** Natives and Exotics

**Alvarez, Julia.** In the Name of Salome

**Alvarez, Julia.** In the Time of the Butterflies

**Alvord, Lori** and **Van Pelt, Elizabeth Cohen.** The Scalpel and the Silver Bear: The First Navajo Woman Surgeon Combines Western Medicine and Traditional Healing

**Amatuzio, Janis.** Forever Ours

**Angelou, Maya.** I Know Why the Caged Bird Sings

**Arana, Marie.** American Chica: Two Worlds, One Childhood

**Arana, Marie.** Cellophane

**Arnow, Harriette.** The Dollmaker

**Arrien, Angeles.** The Four-Fold Way: Walking the Paths of Warrior, Teacher, Healer and Visionary

**Atwood, Margaret.** Alias Grace

**Atwood, Margaret.** Cat's Eye

**Atwood, Margaret.** The Handmaid's Tale

**Atwood, Margaret.** Moral Disorder

**Atwood, Margaret.** Oryx & Crake

**Atwood, Margaret.** The Robber Bride

**Atwood, Margaret.** Selected Poems: 1965-1975

**Atwood, Margaret.** Surfacing

**Austin, Mary.** Cactus Thorn: A Novella

**Austin, Mary.** The Land of Little Rain

**Babb, Sanora.** An Owl on Every Post

**Bair, Deirdre.** Simone de Beauvoir: A Biography

**Baldwin, Christina.** Life's Companion: Journal Writing as a Spiritual Quest

**Barker, Elspeth.** O Caledonia

**Barr, Roseanne.** Roseanne: My Life as a Woman

**Barrington, Judith** (ed). An Intimate Wilderness: Lesbian Writers on Sexuality

**Benítez, Sandra.** A Place Where the Sea Remembers

**Benítez, Sandra.** Bitter Grounds

**Bernikow, Louise.** Among Women

**Blum, Arlene.** Annapurna: A Woman's Place

**Bradley, Marion Zimmer.** The Mists of Avalon

**Brand, Christianna.** Green for Danger

**Brandeis, Gail.** The Book of Dead Birds

**Broner, E.M.** A Weave of Women

**Brontë, Charlotte.** Jane Eyre

**Brooks, Geraldine.** Nine Parts of Desire: The Hidden Life of Islamic Women

**Brooks, Geraldine.** Year of Wonders

**Bruchac, Carol, Linda Hogan, and Judith McDaniels,** (eds). The Stories We Hold Secret: Tales of Women's Spiritual Development

**Bryant, Dorothy.** Confessions of Madame Psyche

**Buchwald, Emilie, Pamela Fletcher, and Martha Roth,** (eds). Transforming a Rape Culture

**Buck, Pearl S.** Pavilion of Women

**Burnett, Frances Hodgson.** The Secret Garden

**Burns, Olive Ann.** Cold Sassy Tree

**Burton, Betsy.** King's English: Adventures of an Independent Bookseller

**Butala, Sharon.** Luna

**Butler, Octavia.** Kindred

**Butler, Octavia.** Parable of the Sower

**Byatt, A.S.** Possession: A Romance

**Calof, Rachel.** Rachel Calof's Story: Jewish Homesteader on the Northern Plains

**Cameron, Anne.** Daughters of Copper Woman

**Cameron, Julia.** The Artist's Way: A Spiritual Path to Higher Creativity

**Campbell, Alla Bozarth.** Life is Goodbye, Life is Hello: Grieving Well Through All Kinds of Loss

**Canfield, Dorothy.** The Home-Maker

**Carson, Rachel.** The Edge of the Sea

**Carson, Rachel.** Silent Spring

**Cather, Willa.** Death Comes for the Archbishop

**Cather, Willa.** Lucy Gayheart

**Cather, Willa.** My Antonia

**Cather, Willa.** O Pioneers!

**Cather, Willa.** The Song of the Lark

**Chang, Jung.** Wild Swans: Three Daughters Of China

**Cheng, Nien.** Life and Death in Shanghai

**Chernin, Kim.** Re-Inventing Eve: Modern Woman in Search of Herself

**Chevalier, Tracy.** Girl with a Pearl Earring

**Church, Peggy Pond.** The House at Otowi Bridge: The Story of Edith Warner and Los Alamos

**Christ, Carol.** Laughter of Aphrodite: Reflections on a Journey to the Goddess

**Christ, Carol.** Womanspirit Rising: A Feminist Reader in Religion

**Cisneros, Sandra.** Caramelo

**Cline, Sally.** Women, Passion and Celibacy

**Cody, Lisa.** Rift

**Conway, Jill Ker.** The Road From Coorain

**Cook, Blanche Wiesen.** Eleanor Roosevelt, Volume One: 1884-1933

**Cooley, Martha.** The Archivist

**Craighead, Meinrad.** The Mother's Songs: Images of God the Mother

**Crombie, Deborah.** Dreaming of the Bones

**Daly, Mary.** Gyn-Ecology: The Metaethics of Radical Feminism

**Daly, Mary.** Outercourse: The Be-Dazzling Voyage

**Daly, Mary.** Pure Lust: Elemental Feminist Philosophy

**Dangarembga, Tsitsi.** Nervous Conditions

**Danticat, Edwidge.** The Farming of Bones

**Davidson, Cathy.** 36 Views of Mount Fuji

**Day, Marele.** Lambs of God

**DeBlieu, Jan.** Hatteras Journal

**Delany, Sarah and A. Elizabeth, with Amy Hill Hearth.** Having Our Say: The Delany Sisters' First 100 Years

**Desai, Kiran.** The Inheritance of Loss

**Diamant, Anita.** The Red Tent

**Dillard, Annie.** Teaching a Stone to Talk: Expeditions and Encounters

**Dorner, Marjorie.** Winter Roads, Summer Fields

**Dressler, Mylene.** The Deadwood Beetle

**Duerk, Judith** (ed). Circle of Stones: Woman's Journey to Herself

**Dunn, Katherine.** Geek Love

**Ehrenreich, Barbara and English, Deirdre.** For Her Own Good: 150 Years of the Experts' Advice to Women

**Ehrenreich, Barbara.** Nickel and Dimed: On (Not) Getting By in America

**Eisler, Riane.** The Chalice and The Blade: Our History, Our Future

**Eisler, Riane.** Sacred Pleasure

**Elgin, Suzette.** Native Tongue

**Erdrich, Louise.** Books and Islands in Ojibwe Country

**Erdrich, Louise.** Four Souls

**Erdrich, Louise.** The Last Report on the Miracles at Little No Horse

**Erdrich, Louise.** Love Medicine

**Erdrich, Louise.** The Master Butchers Singing Club

**Erdrich, Louise.** The Painted Drum

**Erdrich, Louise.** Tales of Burning Love

**Erdrich, Louise.** The Blue Jay's Dance

**Esquivel, Laura.** Like Water For Chocolate

**Estés, Clarissa Pinkola.** Women Who Run With the Wolves: Myths and Stories of the Wild Woman Archetype

**Faderman, Lillian.** Odd Girls and Twilight Lovers: A History of Lesbian Life in Twentieth-Century America

**Faderman, Lillian.** Surpassing the Love of Men: Romantic Friendship and Love Between Women From the Renaissance to the Present

**Fadiman, Anne.** Ex Libris: Confessions of a Common Reader

**Fadiman, Anne.** The Spirit Catches You and You Fall Down

**Faludi, Susan.** Backlash: The Undeclared War Against American Women

**Ferré, Rosario.** Eccentric Neighborhoods

**Fink, Augusta.** I-Mary: A Biography of Mary Austin

**Fink, Ida.** The Journey

**Fitch, Janet.** White Oleander

**Flagg, Fannie.** Fried Green Tomatoes at the Whistle Stop Cafe

**Floyd, Patty Lou.** The Silver DeSoto

**Fonseca, Isabel.** Bury Me Standing: The Gypsies and Their Journey

**Frame, Janet.** Janet Frame: An Autobiography

**Forbes, Edith.** Alma Rose

## Gág, Wanda. Growing Pains

**Galford, Ellen.** The Fires of Bride

**Gawain, Shakti.** Living in the Light: A Guide to Personal and Planetary Transformation

**Gelman, Rita Golden.** Tales of a Female Nomad: Living at Large in the World

**Gershten, Donna.** Kissing the Virgin's Mouth

**Gilman, Charlotte Perkins.** The Yellow Wallpaper

**Gilligan, Carol.** In a Different Voice: Psychological Theory and Women's Development

**Glass, Julia.** Three Junes

**Godden, Rumer.** Kingfishers Catch Fire

**Godwin, Gail.** The Finishing School

**Goldberg, Myla.** Bee Season

**Gordimer, Nadine.** July's People

**Gordimer, Nadine.** None to Accompany Me

**Gordimer, Nadine.** The Pickup

**Gordon, Mary.** Spending: A Utopian Divertimento

**Grace, Patricia.** Potiki

**Graver, Elizabeth.** Unraveling

**Grealy, Lucy.** Autobiography of a Face

**Griffin, Susan.** A Chorus Of Stones: The Private Life of War

**Griffin, Susan.** Pornography and Silence: Culture's Revolt Against Nature

**Griffin, Susan.** Woman and Nature: The Roaring Inside Her

**Grumbach, Doris.** Chamber Music

**Grumbach, Doris.** Extra Innings: A Memoir

**Grumbach, Doris.** The Ladies

**Gunnars, Kristiana.** The Prowler

## Hall, Sarah. Haweswater

**Hampl, Patricia.** A Romantic Education

**Hamilton, Jane.** A Map of the World

**Hamilton, Jane.** The Short History of a Prince

**Hancock, Emily.** The Girl Within: A Groundbreaking New Approach to Female Identity

**Hanff, Helene.** 84, Charing Cross Road

**Harris, Joanne.** Chocolat

**Hathaway, Katharine Butler.** The Little Locksmith: A Memoir

**Haushofer, Marlen.** The Wall

**Hegi, Ursula.** Stones From the River

**Hegland, Jean.** Into the Forest: A Novel

**Heilbrun, Carolyn.** The Last Gift of Time: Life Beyond Sixty

**Heilbrun, Carolyn.** Writing a Woman's Life

**Helmericks, Constance.** Down the Wild River North

**Henley, Patricia.** Hummingbird House

**Herrera, Hayden.** Frida: A Biography of Frida Kahlo

**Hoffman, Eva.** Lost in Translation: A Life in a New Language

**Hogan, Linda.** Dwellings: A Spiritual History of the Living World

**Hogan, Linda and Peterson, Brenda (eds.).** Face to Face: Women Writers on Faith, Mysticism, and Awakening

**Hogan, Linda.** Mean Spirit

**Hogan, Linda.** Solar Storms

**Hogan, Linda.** The Woman Who Watches Over the World

**Holdstock, Pauline.** Burial Ground

**Holleman, Marybeth.** Heart of the Sound

**Holman, Sheri.** The Dress Lodger

**Horvath, Polly.** Canning Season

**Hudson, Lois Phillips.** Bones of Plenty

**Hubbard, Ruth and Randall, Margaret.** Shape of Red: Insider-Outsider Reflections

**Hulme, Keri.** The Bone People

**Hurston, Zora Neale.** Their Eyes Were Watching God

**Hustvedt, Siri.** What I Loved

**Jiles, Paulette.** Enemy Women

**Jiles, Paulette.** North Spirit: Sojourns Among the Cree and Ojibway

**Joern, Pamela Carter.** The Floor of the Sky

**Johnson, Josephine.** Now in November

**Johnson, Sonia.** Going Out of Our Minds: The Metaphysics of Liberation

**Johnson, Sonia.** The Ship That Sailed into the Living Room: Sex and Intimacy Reconsidered

**Johnson, Sonia.** Wildfire: Igniting the She/Volution

**Johnston, Tracy.** Shooting the Boh: A Woman's Voyage Down the Wildest River in Borneo

**Jolley, Elizabeth.** The Well

**Jones, Ann.** Looking for Lovedu: A Woman's Journey Across Africa

**Jones, Kathleen.** A Passionate Sisterhood: Women of the Wordsworth Circle

**Joseph, Lynn.** The Color of My Words

**Kidd, Sue Monk.** Dance of the Dissident Daughter: A Woman's Journey from Christian Tradition to the Sacred Feminine.

**Kingsolver, Barbara.** Animal Dreams

**Kingsolver, Barbara.** The Bean Trees

**Kingsolver, Barbara.** High Tide in Tucson: Essays from Now or Never

**Kingsolver, Barbara.** Holding the Line: Women in the Great Arizona Mine Strike of 1983

**Kingsolver, Barbara.** Pigs in Heaven

**Kingsolver, Barbara.** The Poisonwood Bible

**Kingsolver, Barbara.** Prodigal Summer

**Kingsolver, Barbara.** Small Wonder

**Kingston, Maxine Hong.** Woman Warrior: Memoirs of a Girlhood Among Ghosts

**Kohl, Edith Eudora.** Land of the Burnt Thigh

**Kohzina, Elena.** Through the Burning Steppe: A Memoir of Wartime Russia, 1942-1943

**Koller, Alice.** An Unknown Woman: A Journey to Self Discovery

**Konecky, Edith.** Allegra Maud Goldman

**Krauss, Nicole.** The History of Love

**LaBastille, Anne.** Women and Wilderness

**Lahiri, Jhumpa.** The Namesake

**Lamott, Anne.** Bird by Bird: Some Instructions on Writing and Life.

**Landsman, Anne.** The Devil's Chimney

**Langton, Jane.** Dark Nantucket Noon

**Laurence, Margaret.** The Stone Angel

**Lear, Linda.** Rachel Carson: Witness for Nature

**Lee, Hermione.** Virginia Woolf

**Leffland, Ella.** Breath and Shadows

**Le Guin, Ursula K.** Always Coming Home

**Le Guin, Ursula K.** Lao Tzu Tao Te Ching: A Book About the Way and the Power of the Way

**Le Guin, Ursula K.** The Telling

**Le Guin, Ursula K.** The Wave in the Mind: Talks and Essays on the Writer, the Reader, and the Imagination

**Lerner, Gerda.** The Creation of Patriarchy

**Levi, Jan Heller** (ed). A Muriel Rukeyser Reader

**Levy, Andrea.** Small Island

**Lindbergh, Anne Morrow.** Gift From the Sea

**Lippard, Lucy.** Overlay: Contemporary Art and the Art of Prehistory

**Lively, Penelope.** Moon Tiger

**Lorde, Audre.** Sister Outsider: Essays & Speeches

**Lorde, Audre.** Uses of the Erotic: The Erotic as Power

**Lorde, Audre.** Zami: A New Spelling of My Name

**Lowry, Lois.** Gathering Blue

**Lowry, Lois.** The Giver

**Luhan, Mabel Dodge.** Winter in Taos

**Lyden, Jacki.** Daughter of the Queen of Sheba

**MacDonald, Anne-Marie.** Fall on Your Knees
**Mairs, Nancy.** Waist-High in the World: A Life Among the Nondisabled
**Maitland, Sara.** Ancestral Truths
**Maitland, Sara.** Three Times Table
**Markham, Beryl.** West With the Night
**Marriott, Alice.** Maria: The Potter of San Ildefonso
**Martin, Valerie.** Property
**Martinac, Paula.** Out of Time
**McCrumb, Sharyn.** She Walks These Hills
**McCullers, Carson.** The Heart is a Lonely Hunter
**McDermid, Val.** Place of Execution
**Meigs, Mary.** In the Company of Strangers
**Meloy, Ellen.** Raven's Exile: A Season on the Green River
**Meyers, Margaret.** Swimming in the Congo
**Michaels, Anne.** Fugitive Pieces
**Millett, Kate.** The Loony-Bin Trip
**Min, Anchee.** Red Azalea
**Minatoya, Lydia.** Talking to High Monks in the Snow: An Asian-American Odyssey
**Moffat, Mary Jane and Painter, Charlotte** (eds). Revelations: Diaries of Women
**Moon, Elizabeth,** The Speed of Dark
**Moore, Kathleen Dean.** Riverwalking: Reflections on Moving Water
**Moore, Ruth.** Spoonhandle
**Morehouse, Lyda.** Archangel Protocol
**Moriarty, Laura.** The Center of Everything
**Morrison, Toni.** Beloved
**Morrison, Toni.** The Bluest Eye
**Morrison, Toni.** Paradise
**Morrison, Toni.** Sula
**Murdoch, Iris.** The Sea, The Sea
**Murphy, Dervla.** Full Tilt: Ireland to India with a Bicycle

**Namu, Yang Erche.** Leaving Mother Lake: A Girlhood at the Edge of the World
**Nahai, Gina.** Moonlight on the Avenue of Faith
**Naslund, Sena Jeter.** Ahab's Wife

**Naylor, Gloria.** Bailey's Cafe
**Naylor, Gloria.** Mama Day
**Neely, Barbara.** Blanche on the Lam
**Nemirovsky, Irene.** Suite Française
**Niffenegger, Audrey.** The Time Traveler's Wife
**Niven, Jennifer.** Ada Blackjack: A True Story of Survival in the Arctic
**Norris, Kathleen.** Dakota: A Spiritual Geography
**Nzenza-Shand, Sekai.** Songs to an African Sunset: A Zimbabwean Story.

**O'Connor, Sheila.** Where No Gods Came
**Olsen, Tillie.** Silences
**Otsuka, Julie.** When the Emperor Was Divine
**Ozeki, Ruth.** All Over Creation
**Ozeki, Ruth.** My Year of Meats
**Ozick, Cynthia.** Heir to the Glimmering World

**Padgett, Abigail.** Child of Silence
**Paley, Grace and Williams, Vera.** Long Walks, Intimate Talks
**Paretsky, Sara.** Bitter Medicine
**Paretsky, Sara.** Blood Shot
**Paretsky, Sara.** Guardian Angel
**Patchett, Ann.** Bel Canto
**Patchett, Ann.** The Magician's Assistant
**Patchett, Ann.** Truth and Beauty
**Piercy, Marge.** Gone to Soldiers
**Piercy, Marge.** He, She and It
**Piercy, Marge.** The Longings of Women
**Piercy, Marge.** Summer People
**Piercy, Marge.** Woman on the Edge of Time
**Plant, Judith** (ed). Healing the Wounds: The Promise of Ecofeminism
**Plaskow, Judith and Christ, Carol** (eds). Weaving the Visions: Patterns in Feminist Spirituality
**Plath, Sylvia.** The Bell Jar
**Popham, Melinda Worth.** Skywater
**Proulx, E. Annie.** Accordion Crimes
**Proulx, E. Annie.** The Shipping News

**Q**uindlen, **Anna.** One True Thing

**R**afkin, **Louise** (ed). Different Daughters: A Book by Mothers of Lesbians

**Rafkin, Louise** (ed). Different Mothers: Sons and Daughters of Lesbians Talk About Their Lives

**Rafkin, Louise** (ed). Unholy Alliances: New Fiction by Women

**Ramsland, Katherine.** Prism of the Night: A Biography of Anne Rice

**Rich, Adrienne.** What Is Found There: Notebooks in Poetry and Politics

**Robinson, Eden.** Monkey Beach

**Robinson, Marilynne.** Housekeeping

**Rostenberg, Leona and Stern, Madeleine.** Old Books, Rare Friends: Two Literary Sleuths and Their Shared Passion

**Rowling, J. K.** Harry Potter and the Half-Blood Prince

**Roy, Arundhati.** The God of Small Things

**Ruebsamen, Helga.** The Song and the Truth

**Ruddick, Sara.** Maternal Thinking: Toward a Politics of Peace

**Russell, Mary Doria.** Children of God

**S**acher, **Louis.** Holes

**Sackville-West, Vita.** All Passion Spent

**Sapphire.** Push

**Sarton, Eleanor Mabel.** Letters to May

**Sarton, May.** Crucial Conversations

**Sarton, May.** The Education of Harriet Hatfield

**Sarton, May.** Journal of a Solitude

**Satrapi, Marjane.** Persepolis: The Story of Childhood

**Savage, Georgia.** The House Tibet

**Sayers, Dorothy.** Gaudy Night

**Schaef, Anne Wilson.** Women's Reality: An Emerging Female System in the White Male Society

**Schreiner, Olive.** The Story of an African Farm

**See, Lisa.** Snow Flower and the Secret Fan

**Seierstad, Asne.** The Bookseller of Kabul

**Sebold, Alice.** The Lovely Bones

**Sharratt, Mary.** The Real Minerva

**Sharp, Paula.** I Loved You All

**Shelley, Mary.** Frankenstein

**Shields, Carol.** The Stone Diaries

**Shin, Nan.** Diary of a Zen Nun: Everyday Living

**Shulman, Alix Kates.** Drinking the Rain

**Shuttle, Penelope and Peter Redgrove.** The Wise Wound: Myths, Realities and Meanings of Menstruation

**Shriver, Lionell.** We Need to Talk About Kevin

**Signell, Karen.** Wisdom of the Heart: Working With Women's Dreams

**Sigurdardottir, Frida.** Night Watch

**Silko, Leslie Marmon.** Almanac of the Dead

**Silko, Leslie Marmon.** Ceremony

**Silko, Leslie Marmon.** Yellow Woman and a Beauty of the Spirit: Essays on Native American Life Today

**Sinclair, Jo.** The Changelings

**Sjoo, Monica and Mor, Barbara.** The Great Cosmic Mother: Rediscovering the Religion of the Earth

**Slonczewski, Joan.** Brain Plauge

**Slonczewski, Joan.** Daughter of Elysium

**Smedley, Agnes.** Daughter of Earth

**Smiley, Jane.** A Thousand Acres

**Smith, Diane.** Letters from Yellowstone

**Smith, Zadie.** On Beauty

**Smith, Zadie.** White Teeth

**Soueif, Ahdaf.** Map of Love

**Souhami, Diana.** Gertrude and Alice

**Spark, Muriel.** The Driver's Seat.

**Stabenow, Dana.** A Cold Day for Murder

**Starhawk.** Dreaming the Dark: Magic, Sex and Politics

**Stein, Diane** (ed). The Goddess Celebrates: An Anthology of Women's Rituals

**Steinem, Gloria.** Revolution From Within: A Book of Self-Esteem

**Stern, Madeleine & Rostenberg, Leona.** Old Books, Rare Friends: Two Literary Sleuths and Their Shared Passion

**Straight, Susan.** Highwire Moon
**Straight, Susan.** I Been in Sorrow's Kitchen and Licked Out All the Pots
**Sullivan, Faith.** The Cape Ann
**Sullivan, Faith.** The Empress of One

**T**an, Amy. The Hundred Secret Senses
**Tannen, Deborah.** You Just Don't Understand: Women and Men in Conversation
**Taylor, Katherine Kressmann.** Address Unknown
**Tepper, Sheri.** Companions
**Tepper, Sheri.** The Family Tree
**Tepper, Sheri.** The Fresco
**Tepper, Sheri.** Gate to Women's Country
**Tepper, Sheri.** Gibbon's Decline and Fall
**Tepper, Sheri.** Raising the Stones
**Tepper, Sheri.** Singer from the Sea
**Tey, Josephine.** Daughter of Time
**Thomson, Amy.** Color of Distance
**Trapido, Barbara.** The Travelling Hornplayer
**Truong, Monique.** The Book of Salt
**Tsukiyama, Gail.** The Samurai's Garden
**Tsukiyama, Gail.** Women of the Silk
**Turner, Nancy.** These Is My Words: The Diary of Sarah Agnes Prine, 1881-1901 Arizona Territories

**U**eland, Brenda. Me: A Memoir
**Ueland, Brenda.** Strength to Your Sword Arm: Selected Writings
**Umrigar, Thrity.** The Space Between Us
**Underhill, Ruth M.** Papago Woman

**V**on Herzen, Lane. Copper Crown
**Vowell, Sarah.** Assassination Vacation
**Vreeland, Susan.** The Forest Lover

**W**agner, Jane. The Search for Signs of Intelligent Life in the Universe
**Walker, Alice.** Anything We Love Can Be Saved: A Writer's Activism
**Walker, Alice.** The Color Purple

**Walker, Alice.** In Search of Our Mother's Gardens: Womanist Prose
**Walker, Alice.** Possessing the Secret of Joy
**Walker, Alice.** The Temple of My Familiar
**Walker, Barbara.** The Crone: Woman of Age, Wisdom and Power
**Walker, Barbara.** The Skeptical Feminist: Discovering the Virgin, Mother, Crone
**Walker, Mary Willis.** Under the Beetle's Cellar
**Walker, Rebecca.** To Be Real: Telling the Truth and Changing the Face of Feminism
**Wallis, Velma.** Bird Girl and the Man Who Followed the Sun: An Athabascan Legend from Alaska
**Wallis, Velma.** Two Old Women: An Alaska Legend of Betrayal, Courage and Survival
**Walls, Jeanette.** The Glass Castle
**Waters, Sara.** Affinity
**Waters, Sara.** Fingersmith
**Weber, Katharine.** Triangle
**Weiss, Andrea.** Paris Was a Woman: Portraits from the Left Bank
**West, Dorothy.** The Wedding
**Wharton, Edith.** Ethan Frome
**Wiggins, Marianne.** Evidence of Things Unseen
**Williams, Terry Tempest.** Red: Passion and Patience in the Desert
**Williams, Terry Tempest.** Refuge: An Unnatural History of Family and Place
**Winterson, Jeannette.** Written on the Body
**Wong, Jan.** Red China Blues: My Long March from Mao to Now
**Woolf, Virginia.** A Room of One's Own
**Woolf, Virginia.** Mrs. Dalloway

**Y**olen, Jane. Sister Light, Sister Dark

**Z**usak, Markus. The Book Thief

# By Genre

*You'll see that—in the spirit with which we have redefined the term "Great Books"—we've created different genres for classifying the books, ones that better reflect the experiences and reactions of the many readers who chose them. Some books may appear in more than one genre.*

## ADVENTURE
*Adding a thrill to life.*

**Annapurna: A Woman's Place,** Arlene Blum

**Books and Islands in Ojibwe Country,** Louise Erdrich

**Down the Wild River North,** Constance Helmericks

**Full Tilt: Ireland to India with a Bicycle,** Dervla Murphy

**Looking for Lovedu: A Woman's Journey Across Africa,** Ann Jones

**Shooting the Boh: A Woman's Voyage Down the Wildest River in Borneo,** Tracy Johnston

**Tales of a Female Nomad: Living at Large in the World,** Rita Golden Gelman

**Talking to High Monks in the Snow: An Asian-American Odyssey,** Lydia Minatoya

**Woman and Wilderness,** Anne LaBastille

## ANTHOLOGY, ESSAY, POETRY, NOVELLA & SHORT STORY
*Capturing the essence, providing provocative moments.*

**Anything We Love Can Be Saved: A Writer's Activism,** Alice Walker

**Bird Girl and the Man Who Followed the Sun: An Athabascan Legend from Alaska,** Velma Wallis

**Cactus Thorn: A Novella,** Austin, Mary

**Dakota: A Spiritual Geography,** Kathleen Norris

**Different Daughters: A Book by Mothers of Lesbians,** Louise Rafkin, ed.

**Different Mothers: Sons and Daughters of Lesbians Talk About Their Lives,** Louise Rafkin, ed.

**The Driver's Seat,** Muriel Spark

**Ex Libris: Confessions of a Common Reader,** Anne Fadiman

**Gift from the Sea,** Anne Morrow Lindberg

**The Goddess Celebrates: An Anthology of Women's Rituals,** Diane Stein, ed.

**Healing the Wounds: The Promise of Ecofeminism,** Judith Plant, ed.

**High Tide in Tucson: Essays from Now or Never,** Barbara Kingsolver

**In Search of Our Mother's Gardens: Womanist Prose,** Alice Walker

**An Intimate Wilderness: Lesbian Writers on Sexuality,** Judith Barrington, ed.

**Lao Tzu Tao Te Ching: A Book About the Way and the Power of the Way,** Ursula K. Le Guin

**Long Walks, Intimate Talks,** Grace Paley and Vera Williams

**Moral Disorder,** Margaret Atwood

**A Muriel Rukeyser Reader,** Jan Heller Levi, ed.

**Red: Passion and Patience in the Desert,** Terry Tempest Williams

**A Room of One's Own,** Virginia Woolf

**Selected Poems: 1965-1975,** Margaret Atwood

**Silences,** Tillie Olsen

**Sister Outsider: Essays & Speeches,** Audre Lorde

**Small Wonder,** Barbara Kingsolver

**The Stories We Hold Secret: Tales of Women's Spiritual Development,** Carol Bruchac, Linda Hogan, Judith McDaniels, eds.

**Teaching a Stone to Talk: Expeditions and Encounters,** Annie Dillard

**Two Old Women: An Alaska Legend of Betrayal, Courage and Survival,** Velma Wallis

**Unholy Alliances: New Fiction by Women,**
Louise Rafkin, ed.

**Uses of the Erotic: The Erotic as Power,**
Audre Lorde

**The Wave in the Mind: Talks and Essays on the Writer, the Reader, and the Imagination,**
Ursula K. Le Guin

**Weaving the Visions: Patterns in Feminist Spirituality,** Judith Plaskow and Carol Christ, eds.

**What Is Found There: Notebooks in Poetry and Politics,** Adrienne Rich

**Winter in Taos,** Mabel Dodge Luhan

**Winter Roads, Summer Fields,** Marjorie Dorner

**Women Who Run With the Wolves: Myths and Stories of the Wild Woman Archetype,** Clarissa Pinkola Estés

**The Yellow Wallpaper,** Charlotte Perkins Gilman

**Yellow Woman and a Beauty of the Spirit: Essays on Native American Life Today,** Leslie Marmon Silko

## THE ARTS

*For beauty in our lives.*

**Bel Canto,** Ann Patchett

**The Color of My Words,** Lynn Joseph

**The Forest Lover,** Susan Vreeland

**Frida: A Biography of Frida Kahlo,** Hayden Herrera

**Girl with a Pearl Earring,** Tracy Chevalier

**In the Company of Strangers,** Mary Meigs

**The Mother's Songs, Images of God the Mother,** Meinrad Craighead

**Overlay: Contemporary Art and the Art of Prehistory,** Lucy Lippard

**Paris Was a Woman: Portraits from the Left Bank,** Andrea Weiss

**The Search for Signs of Intelligent Life in the Universe,** Jane Wagner

**The Song of the Lark,** Willa Cather

## BIOGRAPHY, AUTOBIOGRAPHY, MEMOIR, DIARY & LETTERS

*History takes on a different appearance when learned through the reading of women's lives.*

**Ada Blackjack: A True Story of Survival in the Arctic,** Jennifer Niven

**American Chica: Two Worlds, One Childhood,** Marie Arana

**Among Women,** Louise Bernikow

**Aphrodite: A Memoir of the Senses,** Isabel Allende

**Assassination Vacation,** Sarah Vowell

**Autobiography of a Face,** Lucy Grealy

**Bird by Bird: Some Instructions on Writing and Life,** Anne Lamott

**The Blue Jay's Dance,** Louise Erdrich

**Bones of Plenty,** Lois Phillips Hudson

**Books and Islands in Ojibwe Country,** Louise Erdrich

**The Bookseller of Kabul,** Asne Seierstad

**Bury Me Standing: The Gypsies and Their Journey,** Isabel Fonseca

**Daughter of the Queen of Sheba,** Jacki Lyden

**Diary of a Zen Nun: Everyday Living,** Nan Shin

**Drinking the Rain,** Alix Kates Shulman

**84, Charing Cross Road,** Helene Hanff

**Eleanor Roosevelt, Volume One: 1884-1933,** Blanche Wiesen Cook

**Extra Innings: A Memoir,** Doris Grumbach

**Face to Face: Women Writers on Faith, Mysticism and Awakening,** eds. Linda Hogan and Brenda Peterson, eds.

**Frida: A Biography of Frida Kahlo,** Hayden Herrera

**The Glass Castle,** Jeannette Walls

**Gertrude and Alice,** Diana Souhami

**Growing Pains,** Wanda Gág

**Hatteras Journal,** Jan DeBlieu

**Having Our Say: The Delany Sisters' First 100 Years,** Sarah and A. Elizabeth Delany, with Amy Hill Hearth

**The Heart of the Sound,** Marybeth Holleman

Holding the Line: Women in the Great Arizona Mine Strike of 1983, Barbara Kingsolver

The House at Otowi Bridge: The Story of Edith Warner and Los Alamos, Peggy Pond Church

I Know Why the Caged Bird Sings, Maya Angelou

I-Mary: A Biography of Mary Austin, Augusta Fink

Janet Frame: An Autobiography, Janet Frame

Journal of a Solitude, May Sarton

Land of the Burnt Thigh, Edith Eudora Kohl

The Last Gift of Time: Life Beyond Sixty, Carolyn Heilbrun

Leaving Mother Lake: A Girlhood at the Edge of the World, Yang Erche Namu

Letters to May, Eleanor Mabel Sarton

Life and Death in Shanghai, Nien Cheng

The Little Locksmith: A Memoir, Katharine Butler Hathaway

Looking for Lovedu: A Woman's Journey Across Africa, Ann Jones

The Loony-Bin Trip, Kate Millett

Lost in Translation: A Life in a New Language, Eva Hoffman

Madam Secretary, Madeleine Albright

Maria: The Potter of San Ildefonso, Alice Marriott

Me: A Memoir, Brenda Ueland

North Spirit: Sojourns Among the Cree and Ojibway, Paulette Jiles

Old Books, Rare Friends: Two Literary Sleuths and Their Shared Passion, Leona Rostenberg & Madeleine Stern

An Owl on Every Post, Sanora Babb

Papago Woman, Ruth M. Underhill

Paris Was a Woman: Portraits from the Left Bank, Andrea Weiss

A Passionate Sisterhood: Women of the Wordsworth Circle, Kathleen Jones

Paula, Isabel Allende

Persepolis: The Story of Childhood, Marjane Satrapi

Prism of the Night: A Biography of Anne Rice, Katherine Ramsland

Rachel Calof's Story: Jewish Homesteader on the Northern Plains, Rachel Calof

Rachel Carson: Witness for Nature, Linda Lear

Red: Passion and Patience in the Desert, Terry Tempest Williams

Red Azalea, Anchee Min

Red China Blues: My Long March from Mao to Now, Jan Wong

Refuge: An Unnatural History of Family and Place, Terry Tempest Williams

Revelations: Diaries of Women, Mary Jane Moffat and Charlotte Painter, eds.

Revolution From Within: A Book of Self-Esteem, Gloria Steinem

Riverwalking: Reflections on Moving Water, Kathleen Dean Moore

The Road From Coorain, Jill Ker Conway

A Romantic Education, Patricia Hampl

Roseanne: My Life as a Woman, Roseanne Barr

The Scalpel and the Silver Bear: The First Navajo Woman Surgeon Combines Western Medicine and Traditional Healing, Lori Alvord and Elizabeth Cohen Van Pelt

Shooting the Boh: A Woman's Voyage Down the Wildest River in Borneo, Tracy Johnston

Simone de Beauvoir: A Biography, Deirdre Bair

Songs to an African Sunset: A Zimbabwean Story, Sekai Nzenza-Shand

The Spirit Catches You and You Fall Down, Anne Fadiman

Strength to Your Sword Arm: Selected Writings, Brenda Ueland

Tales of a Female Nomad: Living at Large in the World, Rita Golden Gelman

Talking to High Monks in the Snow: An Asian-American Odyssey, Lydia Minatoya

36 Views of Mount Fuji, Cathy Davidson

Through the Burning Steppe: A Memoir of Wartime Russia, 1942-1943, Elena Kohzina

To Be Real: Telling the Truth and Changing the Face of Feminism, Rebecca Walker, ed.

Truth and Beauty, Ann Patchett

An Unknown Woman: A Journey to Self Discovery, Alice Koller

Virginia Woolf, Hermione Lee

Waist-High in the World: A Life Among the Nondisabled, Nancy Mairs

West with the Night, Beryl Markham

Wild Swans: Three Daughters of China, Jung Chang

Winter in Taos, Mabel Dodge Luhan

Woman Warrior: Memoirs of a Girlhood Among Ghosts, Maxine Hong Kingston

The Woman Who Watches Over the World: A Native Memoir, Linda Hogan

Writing A Woman's Life, Carolyn Heilbrun

Yellow Woman and a Beauty of the Spirit: Essays on Native American Life Today, Leslie Marmon Silko

Zami: A New Spelling of My Name, Audre Lorde

## CULTURE CRITIQUE

*These books challenge the status quo.*

Almanac of the Dead, Leslie Marmon Silko

Backlash: The Undeclared War Against American Women, Susan Faludi

Bury Me Standing: The Gypsies and Their Journey, Isabel Fonseca

A Chorus of Stones: The Private Life of War, Susan Griffin

The Creation of Patriarchy, Gerda Lerner

For Her Own Good: 150 Years of the Experts' Advice to Women, Barbara Ehrenreich and Deirdre English

Forever Ours, Janis Amatuzio

The Girl Within: A Groundbreaking New Approach to Female Identity, Emily Hancock

Going Out of Our Minds: The Metaphysics of Liberation, Sonia Johnson

Gyn-Ecology: The Metaethics of Radical Feminism, Mary Daly

Hatteras Journal, Jan DeBlieu

Holding the Line: Women in the Great Arizona Mine Strike of 1983, Barbara Kingsolver

In a Different Voice: Psychological Theory and Women's Development, Carol Gilligan

Maternal Thinking: Toward a Politics of Peace, Sara Ruddick

Nickel and Dimed: On (Not) Getting By in America, Barbara Ehrenreich

Nine Parts of Desire: The Hidden World of Islamic Women, Geraldine Brooks

Odd Girls and Twilight Lovers: A History of Lesbian Life in Twentieth-Century America, Lillian Faderman

Outercourse: The Be-Dazzling Voyage, Mary Daly

Pornography and Silence: Culture's Revolt Against Nature, Susan Griffin

Pure Lust: Elemental Feminist Philosophy, Mary Daly

A Room of One's Own, Virginia Woolf

The Scalpel and the Silver Bear: The First Navajo Woman Surgeon Combines Western Medicine and Traditional Healing, Lori Alvord and Elizabeth Cohen Van Pelt

Shape of Red: Insider-Outsider Reflections, Ruth Hubbard and Margaret Randall

The Ship that Sailed into the Living Room: Sex and Intimacy Reconsidered, Sonia Johnson

Silences, Tillie Olsen

Silent Spring, Rachel Carson

Sister Outsider: Essays & Speeches, Audre Lorde

Surpassing the Love of Men: Romantic Friendship and Love Between Women from the Renaissance to the Present, Lillian Faderman

To Be Real: Telling the Truth and Changing the Face of Feminism, Rebecca Walker, ed.

Transforming a Rape Culture, Emile Buchwald, Pamela Fletcher, and Martha Roth, eds.

Uses of the Erotic: The Erotic as Power, Audre Lorde

Wildfire: Igniting the She/Volution, Sonia Johnson

The Wise Wound: Myths, Realities and Meanings of Menstruation, Penelope Shuttle and Peter Redgrove

Woman and Nature: The Roaring Inside Her, Susan Griffin

**Women, Passion and Celibacy.** Sally Cline

**Women's Reality: An Emerging Female System in the White Male Society,** Anne Wilson Schaef

**You Just Don't Understand: Women and Men in Conversation,** Deborah Tannen

## MYSTERIES

*For a quick escape, try mysteries.*

**Bitter Medicine,** Sara Paretsky

**Blanche on the Lam,** Barbara Neely

**Blood Shot,** Sara Paretsky

**Child of Silence,** Abigail Padgett

**A Cold Day for Murder,** Dana Stabenow

**Dark Nantucket Noon,** Jane Langton

**The Daughter of Time,** Josephine Tey

**Dreaming of the Bones,** Deborah Crombie

**Gaudy Night,** Dorothy Sayers

**Green for Danger,** Christianna Brand

**Guardian Angel,** Sara Paretsky

**Place of Execution,** Val McDermid

**Rift,** Lisa Cody

**She Walks These Hills,** Sharyn McCrumb

**Under the Beetle's Cellar,** Mary Willis Walker

## NATURE

*Honoring this earth on which we live.*

**Annapurna: A Woman's Place,** Arlene Blum

**Books and Islands in Ojibwe Country,** Louise Erdrich

**Cactus Thorn: A Novella,** Mary Austin

**Down the Wild River North,** Constance Helmericks

**Drinking the Rain,** Alix Kates Shulman

**Dwellings: A Spiritual History of the Living World,** Linda Hogan

**The Edge of the Sea,** Rachel Carson

**Gift from the Sea,** Anne Morrow Lindberg

**The Heart of the Sound,** Marybeth Holleman

**Healing the Wounds: The Promise of Ecofeminism,** Judith Plant, ed.

**The Land of Little Rain,** Mary Austin

**Letters from Yellowstone,** Diane Smith

**Natives and Exotics,** Jane Allison

**An Owl on Every Post,** Sanora Babb

**Pornography and Silence: Culture's Revolt Against Nature,** Susan Griffin

**Prodigal Summer,** Barbara Kingsolver

**Rachel Carson: Witness for Nature,** Linda Lear

**Raven's Exile: A Season on the Green River,** Ellen Meloy

**Red: Passion and Patience in the Desert,** Terry Tempest Williams

**Refuge: An Unnatural History of Family and Place,** Terry Tempest Williams

**Riverwalking: Reflections on Moving Water,** Kathleen Dean Moore

**Silences,** Tillie Olsen

**Silent Spring,** Rachel Carson

**Skywater,** Melinda Worth Popham

**The Song and the Truth,** Helga Ruebsamen

**Teaching a Stone to Talk,** Annie Dillard

**Woman and Nature: The Roaring Inside Her,** Susan Griffin

**The Woman Who Watches Over the World: A Native Memoir,** Linda Hogan

**Women and Wilderness: Expeditions and Encounters,** Anne LaBastille

## NOVELS

*Women read novels more than any other genre. How about you?*

**Accordion Crimes,** E. Annie Proulx

**Address Unknown,** Kathrine Kressmann Taylor

**Affinity,** Sara Waters

**Ahab's Wife,** Sena Jeter Naslund

**Alias Grace,** Margaret Atwood

**All Over Creation,** Ruth Ozeki

**All Passion Spent,** Vita Sackville-West

**Allegra Maud Goldman,** Edith Konecky

**Alma Rose,** Edith Forbes

**Almanac of the Dead,** Leslie Marmon Silko

**Ancestral Truths,** Sara Maitland

**Animal Dreams,** Barbara Kingsolver
**The Archivist,** Martha Cooley
**Bailey's Cafe,** Gloria Naylor
**Bastard Out of Carolina,** Dorothy Allison
**The Bean Trees,** Barbara Kingsolver
**Bee Season,** Myla Goldberg
**Bel Canto,** Ann Patchett
**The Bell Jar,** Sylvia Plath
**Beloved,** Toni Morrison
**Bitter Grounds,** Sandra Benítez
**The Bluest Eye,** Toni Morrison
**The Bone People,** Keri Hulme
**The Book of Dead Birds,** Gayle Brandeis
**The Book of Salt,** Monique Truong
**The Book Thief,** Markus Zusak
**Breath and Shadows,** Ella Leffland
**Burial Ground,** Pauline Holdstock
**The Cactus Thorn,** Mary Austin
**The Canning Season,** Polly Horvath
**The Cape Ann,** Faith Sullivan
**Caramelo,** Sandra Cisneros
**Cat's Eye,** Margaret Atwood
**Cellophane,** Marie Arana
**The Center of Everything,** Laura Moriarty
**Ceremony,** Leslie Marmon Silko
**Chamber Music,** Doris Grumbach
**The Changelings,** Jo Sinclair
**Chocolat,** Joanne Harris
**Cold Sassy Tree,** Olive Ann Burns
**The Color of My Words,** Lynn Joseph
**The Color Purple,** Alice Walker
**Confessions of Madame Psyche,** Dorothy Bryant
**Copper Crown,** Lane Von Herzen
**Crucial Conversations,** May Sarton
**Daughter of Earth,** Agnes Smedley
**The Deadwood Beetle,** Mylene Dressler
**Death Comes for the Archbishop,** Willa Cather
**The Devil's Chimney,** Anne Landsman
**The Dollmaker,** Harriette Arnow
**The Dress Lodger,** Sheri Holman
**The Driver's Seat,** Muriel Spark
**Eccentric Neighborhoods,** Rosario Ferré
**The Education of Harriet Hatfield,** May Sarton

**Ella Minnow Pea,** Mark Dunn
**The Empress of One,** Faith Sullivan
**Enemy Women,** Paulette Giles
**Ethan Frome,** Edith Wharton
**Evidence of Things Unseen,** Marianne Wiggins
**Fall on Your Knees,** Anne-Marie MacDonald
**The Farming of Bones,** Edwidge Danticat
**Fingersmith,** Sarah Waters
**The Finishing School,** Gail Godwin
**The Fires of Bride,** Ellen Galford
**The Floor of the Sky,** Pamela Carta Joern
**The Forest Lover,** Susan Vreeland
**Four Souls,** Louise Erdrich
**Frankenstein,** Mary Shelley
**Fried Green Tomatoes at the Whistle Stop Cafe,** Fannie Flagg
**Fugitive Pieces,** Anne Michaels
**Geek Love,** Katherine Dunn
**Girl with a Pearl Earring,** Tracy Chevalier
**The God of Small Things,** Arundhati Roy
**Gone to Soldiers,** Marge Piercy
**Harry Potter and the Half-Blood Prince,** J.K. Rowling
**Haweswater,** Sarah Hall
**The Heart is a Lonely Hunter,** Carson McCullers
**Heir to the Glimmering World,** Cynthia Ozick
**Highwire Moon,** Susan Straight
**The History of Love,** Nicole Krauss
**The Home-Maker,** Dorothy Canfield
**Holes,** Louis Sacher
**The House Tibet,** Georgia Savage
**Housekeeping,** Marilynne Robinson
**Hummingbird House,** Patricia Henley
**The Hundred Secret Senses,** Amy Tan
**I Been in Sorrow's Kitchen and Licked Out All the Pots,** Susan Straight
**I Loved You All,** Paula Sharp
**In the Name of Salomé,** Julia Alvarez
**In the Time of the Butterflies,** Julia Alvarez
**The Inheritance of Loss,** Anita Desai
**Into the Forest: A Novel,** Jean Hegland
**Jane Eyre,** Charlotte Brontë

The Journey, Ida Fink
July's People, Nadine Gordimer
Kingfishers Catch Fire, Rumer Godden
Kissing the Virgin's Mouth, Donna Gershten
The Ladies, Doris Grumbach
Lambs of God, Marele Day
The Last Report on the Miracles at Little No Horse, Louise Erdrich
Letters from Yellowstone, Diane Smith
Like Water for Chocolate, Laura Esquivel
The Longings of Women, Marge Piercy
Love Medicine, Louise Erdrich
The Lovely Bones, Alice Sebold
Lucy Gayheart, Willa Cather
Luna, Sharon Butala
The Magician's Assistant, Ann Patchett
Mama Day, Gloria Naylor
Map of Love, Ahdaf Soueif
A Map of the World, Jane Hamilton
The Master Butchers Singing Club, Louise Erdrich
Mean Spirit, Linda Hogan
The Mists of Avalon, Marion Zimmer Bradley
Monkey Beach, Eden Robinson
Moon Tiger, Penelope Lively
Moonlight on the Avenue of Faith, Gina Nahai
Mrs. Dalloway, Virginia Woolf
My Antonia, Willa Cather
My Year of Meats, Ruth Ozeki
The Namesake, Jhumpa Lahiri
Natives and Exotics, Jane Allison
Nervous Conditions, Tsitsi Dangarembga
Night Watch, Frida Sigurdardottir
None to Accompany Me, Nadine Gordimer
Now in November, Josephine Johnson
O Caledonia, Elspeth Barker
O Pioneers!, Willa Cather
One True Thing, Anna Quindlen
Oryx & Crake, Margaret Atwood
Out of Time, Paula Martinac
The Painted Drum, Louise Erdrich
Paradise, Toni Morrison
Pavilion of Women, Pearl S. Buck

The Pickup, Nadine Gordimer
Pigs in Heaven, Barbara Kingsolver
A Place Where the Sea Remembers, Sandra Benitez
The Poisonwood Bible, Barbara Kingsolver
Possessing the Secret of Joy, Alice Walker
Possession: A Romance, A.S. Byatt
Potiki, Patricia Grace
Prodigal Summer, Barbara Kingsolver
Property, Valerie Martin
The Prowler, Kristiana Gunnars
Purple Hibiscus, Chimamanda Ngozi Adichie
Push, Sapphire
The Real Minerva, Mary Sharratt
The Red Tent, Anita Diamant
The Robber Bride, Margaret Atwood
The Samurai's Garden, Gail Tsukiyama
The Sea, The Sea, Iris Murdoch
The Secret Garden, Frances Hodgson Burnett
The Shipping News, E. Annie Proulx
The Short History of a Prince, Jane Hamilton
The Silver DeSoto, Patty Lou Floyd
Skywater, Melinda Worth Popham
Small Island, Andrea Levy
Snow Flower and the Secret Fan, Lisa See
Solar Storms, Linda Hogan
The Song and the Truth, Helga Ruebsamen
The Song of the Lark, Willa Cather
The Space Between Us, Thrity Umrigar
Spending: A Utopian Divertimento, Mary Gordon
Spoonhandle, Ruth Moore
The Stone Angel, Margaret Laurence
The Stone Diaries, Carol Shields
Stones From the River, Ursula Hegi
The Story of an African Farm, Olive Schreiner
Suite Française, Irene Nemirovsky
Sula, Toni Morrison
Summer People, Marge Piercy
Surfacing, Margaret Atwood
Swimming in the Congo, Margaret Meyers
Tales of Burning Love, Louise Erdrich
The Temple of My Familiar, Alice Walker

**Their Eyes Were Watching God,** Zora Neale Hurston

**These Is My Words: the Diary of Sarah Agnes Prine 1881-1901, Arizona Territories: A Novel,** Nancy Turner

**Three Junes,** Julia Glass

**Three Times Table,** Sara Maitland

**A Thousand Acres,** Jane Smiley

**The Time Traveler's Wife,** Audrey Niffenegger

**The Travelling Hornplayer,** Barbara Trapido

**Triangle,** Katharine Weber

**Unraveling,** Elizabeth Graver

**The Wall,** Marlen Haushofer

**A Weave of Women,** E.M. Broner

**The Wedding,** Dorothy West

**We Need to Talk About Kevin,** Lionel Shriver

**The Well,** Elizabeth Jolley

**What I Loved,** Siri Hustvedt

**When the Emperor Was Divine,** Julie Otsuka

**Where No Gods Came,** Sheila O'Connor

**White Oleander,** Janet Fitch

**White Teeth,** Zadie Smith

**Woman Warrior: Memoirs of a Girlhood Among Ghosts,** Maxine Hong Kingston

**Women of the Silk,** Gail Tsukiyama

**Written on the Body,** Jeanette Winterson

**Year of Wonders,** Geraldine Brooks

## SCIENCE FICTION/FANTASY

*This is not about spaceships but about possibilities.*

**Always Coming Home,** Ursula K. LeGuin

**Archangel Protocol,** Lyda Morehouse

**Brain Plague,** Joan Slonczewski

**Children of God,** Mary Doria Russell

**Color of Distance,** Amy Thomson

**Companions,** Sheri Tepper

**Daughter of Elysium,** Joan Slonczewski

**The Family Tree,** Sheri Tepper

**The Fresco,** Sheri Tepper

**Gate to Women's Country,** Sheri Tepper

**Gathering Blue,** Lois Lowry

**Gibbon's Decline and Fall,** Sheri Tepper

**The Giver,** Lois Lowry

**The Handmaid's Tale,** Margaret Atwood

**Harry Potter and the Half-Blood Prince,** J. K. Rowling

**He, She and It,** Marge Piercy

**Kindred,** Octavia Butler

**Native Tongue,** Suzette Elgin

**Oryx and Crake,** Margaret Atwood

**Parable of the Sower,** Octavia Butler

**Raising the Stones,** Sheri Tepper

**Sister Light, Sister Dark,** Jane Yolen

**The Speed of Dark,** Elizabeth Moon

**The Telling,** Ursula K. Le Guin

**Woman on the Edge of Time,** Marge Piercy

## SPIRITUALITY

*The journey to one's center follows many paths as one honors being woman.*

**The Artist's Way: A Spiritual Path to Higher Creativity,** Julia Cameron

**The Chalice and the Blade: Our History, Our Future,** Riane Eisler

**Circle of Stones: Woman's Journey to Herself,** Judith Duerk, ed.

**The Crone: Woman of Age, Wisdom and Power,** Barbara Walker

**Dakota: A Spiritual Geography,** Kathleen Norris

**Dance of the Dissident Daughter: A Woman's Journey from Christian Tradition to the Sacred Feminine,** Sue Monk Kidd

**Daughters of Copper Woman,** Anne Cameron

**Diary of a Zen Nun: Everyday Living,** Nan Shin

**Dreaming the Dark: Magic, Sex and Politics,** Starhawk

**Dwellings: A Spiritual History of the Living World,** Linda Hogan

**Face to Face: Women Writers on Faith, Mysicism, and Awakening,** Linda Hogan and Brenda Peterson, eds.

**The Four-Fold Way: Walking the Paths of Warrior, Teacher, Healer and Visionary,** Angeles Arrien

**The Goddess Celebrates: an Anthology of Women's Rituals,** Diane Stein, ed.

**The Great Cosmic Mother: Rediscovering the Religion of the Earth,** Monica Sjoo and Barbara Mor

**Healing the Wounds: The Promise of Ecofeminism,** Judith Plant, ed.

**Lao Tzu Tao Te Ching: A Book About the Way and the Power of the Way,** Ursula K. Le Guin

**Laughter of Aphrodite: Reflections on a Journey to the Goddess,** Carol Christ

**Life is Goodbye, Life is Hello: Grieving Well Through all Kinds of Loss,** Alla Bozarth Campbell

**Life's Companion: Journal Writing as a Spiritual Quest,** Christina Baldwin

**Living in the Light: A Guide to Personal and Planetary Transformation,** Shakti Gawain

**The Mists of Avalon,** Marion Zimmer Bradley

**The Mother's Songs: Images of God the Mother,** Meinrad Craighead

**Re-Inventing Eve: Modern Woman in Search of Herself,** Kim Chernin

**Sacred Pleasure,** Riane Eisler

**The Skeptical Feminist: Discovering the Virgin, Mother, Crone,** Barbara Walker

**The Stories We Hold Secret: Tales of Women's Spiritual Development,** Carol Bruchac, Linda Hogan, Judith McDaniels, eds.

**Teaching a Stone to Talk: Expeditions and Encounters,** Annie Dillard

**Weaving the Visions: Patterns in Feminist Spirituality,** Judith Plaskow & Carol Christ, eds.

**Wisdom of the Heart: Working With Women's Dreams,** Karen Signell

**Womanspirit Rising: A Feminist Reader in Religion,** Carol Christ

**Women Who Run With the Wolves: Myths and Stories of the Wild Woman Archetype,** Clarissa Pinkola Estés

**Yellow Woman and a Beauty of the Spirit: Essays on Native American Life Today,** Leslie Marmon Silko

# BOOK AWARDS

*In the Great Books list, we've indicated titles that have received major literay awards. Here's information about those prizes.*

**Bellwether Prize for Fiction.** Bi-annual prize created by Barbara Kingsolver to support literature of social change.

**Commonwealth Prize,** recognizes fiction written in English by citizens of the British Commonwealth.

**Costa Book Awards,** (formerly the Whitbread Prize). Best novel by an author living in Great Britain or Ireland.

**Giller Prize,** awarded annually for the best Canadian novel or short story collection published in English.

**Governor General's Award,** Canada's oldest and most prestigious award for English- and French-language Canadian literature.

**Kiriyama Pacific Rim Book Prize.** Recognizes books that will contribute to greater understanding among peoples of the Pacific Rim.

**Lambda Literary Award.** Awarded annually in several categories to the best in lesbian and gay writing.

**The Man Booker Prize.** Awarded annually for the best novel written by a citizen of the British Commonweath or the Republic of Ireland.

**National Book Award.** Annual award given by the National Book Foundation for best fiction.

**National Book Critics Circle Award.** Given annually in five categories by U.S. book editors and critics.

**Newbery Medal.** First children's book award, recognizes annually the most distinguished contribution to American literature for children.

**Nordic Council Literary Prize.** Awarded annually for best literary work from the Nordic countries.

**Orange Prize.** Established in 1996 to celebrate the best fiction written in English by women throughout the world.

**Pulitzer Prize for Literature.** Awarded annually for fiction in book form by an American author, preferably dealing with American life.

# GREAT BOOKS FOR CHILDREN OF ALL AGES

*Every reader needs her own collection of children's books. In our Reading Retreats and Book Groups on the Road, and in many book groups, we incorporate children's books whenever possible. Here are a few titles that groups have read together and savored. So many wonderful children's books exist these days, this list is just to get you started.*

## STRONG GIRLS

**Amelia and Eleanor Go for a Ride** by Pam Munoz Ryan, illustrated by Brian Selznick (1999). Honoring the friendship between Amelia Earhart and Eleanor Roosevelt.

**I Like Me** by Nancy Carlson (1988). A charming pig admires her finer points and recalls all the fun she's had being herself.

**I'm a Girl!** by Lila Jukes, illustrated by Susan Keeter (1995). Affirmations of what it means to be a girl.

**Princess Smartypants** by Babette Cole (1986). This is one independent princess.

**Ruby Mae Has Something To Say** by David Small (1992). Ruby Mae speaks for peace.

**Rosie and Michael** by Judith Viorst, illustrated by Lorna Tomei (1974). Two friends share with each other.

**Sheila Rae, the Brave** by Kevin Henkes (1987). Two sisters explore being afraid and being brave.

# CARING BOYS

**I Can Hear the Sun** by Patrica Polacco (1996). The orphan Fondo becomes friends with an animal keeper as together they care for a blind goose who lives by the lake.

**The Lady in the Box** by Ann McGovern, illustrated by Marni Backer (1997). When Ben and Lizzie discover a homeless woman living in their neighborhood, they must reconcile their desire to help with their mother's admonition not to talk to strangers.

**Rosie and Michael** by Judith Viorst, illustrated by Lorna Tomei (1974). Two friends share with each other.

**Wilfred Gordon McDonald Partridge** by Mem Fox, illustrated by Julie Vivas (1985). A boy becomes friends with several elderly folk.

**Willie's Not the Hugging Kind** by Joyce Durham Barrett, illustrated by Pat Cummings (1989). Willie is convinced by his best friend that hugs are silly, but soon he misses hugs and must find a way to become huggable again.

# CONNECTIONS ACROSS CULTURES

**Carly** by Annegert Fuchshuber (1995). A homeless girl finds a home with a fool.

**Dinner at Aunt Connie's House** written and illustrated by Faith Ringgold (1993). At Aunt Connie's house, Melody meets 12 inspiring African-American women, who step out of their portraits and join the family for dinner.

**How My Parents Learned To Eat** by Ina R. Friedman, illustrated by Allen Say (1984). A girl recalls the story of how her Japanese mother learned to eat with silverware and her American father with chopsticks.

**The Serpent Slayer and Other Stories of Strong Women** by Katrin Tchana, illustrated by Trina Schart Human (2000). Tales from around the world, in which the main characters are strong and resourceful women.

**Street Rhymes Around the World** edited by Jane Yolen (1992). Chants and songs sung by children in different nations, with each rhyme illustrated by an artist native to the country.

## CONNECTIONS BETWEEN GENERATIONS

**A Chair for My Mother** by Vera Williams (1982). A daughter, mother and grandmother save dimes to buy a comfortable chair.

**Grandmother's Pigeons** by Louise Erdrich, illustrated by Jim LaMarche (1996). Passenger pigeons are discovered in Grandmother's bedroom after she departs for Greenland on a porpoise.

**How Does It Feel To Be Old?** by Norma Farber, illustrated by Trina Hyman (1979). A grandmother tells with warmth and honesty what it means to get old.

**Just Us Women** by Jeanette Caines, illustrated by Pat Cummings (1982). A girl and her aunt plan a car trip just for the two of them.

**The Table Where Rich People Sit** by Byrd Baylor, illustrated by Peter Parnall (1994). How much is it worth to live the life you desire, close to nature? A girl's parents help her answer this question.

**Wanda's Roses** by Pat Brisson, illustrated by Maryann Cocca-Leffler (1994). Wanda nurtures a bare bush in an empty lot and is nurtured by the adults in her neighborhood.

## EARTH AND ALL LIVING THINGS

**A Story for Bear** by Dennis Haseley, illustrated by Jim LaMarche (2002). Even bears like to have stories read to them.

**Everybody Needs a Rock** by Byrd Baylor, illustrated by Peter Parnall (1974). Each of us needs a rock for peace and security.

**Feathers and Fools** by Mem Fox, illustrated by Nicholas Wilton (1989). Peacocks and swans allow their fear of difference become too great.

**I'm in Charge of Celebrations** by Byrd Baylor, illustrated by Peter Parnall (1986). A daily celebration of life in the southwest desert.

**Insectlopedia** by Douglas Florian (1998). Short, fun poems and illustrations about such insects as the inchworm, termite, cricket and mayfly.

**Miss Rumphius** written and illustrated by Barbara Cooney (1982). Great-aunt Rumphius wished to make the world more beautiful by planting flowers.

**Mole Music** by David McPhail (1999). Mole learns to play the violin and his music has a greater effect on others than he will ever know.

**The Mushroom Man** by Ethel Pochocki, illustrated by Barry Moser (1993). Mushroom man and mole become friends.

**Nurse Lugton's Curtain** by Virginia Woolf, illustrated by Julie Vivas (1982).

**Old Turtle** by Douglas Wood, illustrated by Cheng-Khee Chee (1992). For an understanding of the earth and all the beings who inhabit it.

**On the Day You Were Born** by Debra Frasier (1991). A celebration of the natural world and a welcome to the human family.

**The Other Way to Listen** by Byrd Baylor, illustrated by Peter Parnall (1978). You can hear wildflower seeds burst open when you know "the other way to listen."

## JOY OF LAUGHTER

**Can I Have a Stegosaurus, Mom? Can I? Please!?** by Lois Grambling, illustrated by H.B. Lewis (1995). A little boy imagines the perfect pet.

**Earrings** by Judith Viorst, illustrated by Lola Langner Malone (1993). What's a young girl to do when her parents refuse to let her have her ears pierced?

**Elizabeth and Larry** by Marilyn Sadler, illustrated by Roger Bollen (1990). Elizabeth's best friend is an alligator.

**The Frog Prince Continued** by Jon Scieszka, illustrated by Steve Johnson (1991). The princess kissed the frog. He turned into a prince. And they lived happily ever after...Or did they?

**Hogula: Dread Pig of Night** by Jean Gralley (1999). Hogula goes out to find a friend, and one finds him.

**I Ain't Gonna Paint No More!** by Karen Beaumont (2005). Discover your creative self as you paint—walls, halls, ceilings and doors. As well as head, neck, chest, arm, hand and back. Don't forget legs and feet.

**Never Fear, Snake My Dear!** by Rolf Siegenthaler (1999). A mouse and a snake become friends.

**Purple Hair? I Don't Care!** By Dianne Young, illustrations by Barbara Hartmann (1994). This is one special baby.

**Somebody and the Three Blairs** by Marilyn Tolhurst, illustrated by Simone Abel (1990). A reversal of the story of Goldilocks.

**The Tortoise and the Jackrabbit** by Susan Lowell, illustrated by Jim Harris (1994). A Southwestern take on the "tortoise and the hare."

**The True Story of the 3 Little Pigs!** by Jon Scieszka, illustrated by Lane Smith (1989). The wolf tells his side of the story.

**You Read to Me, I'll Read to You** by Mary Ann Hoberman, illustrations by Michael Emberley (2001). Poetry to read together.

## FOR ALL BOOK LOVERS

**The Library** by Sarah Stewart, illustrated by David Small (1995). In memory of the real Mary Elizabeth Brown, who loved books.

**Library Lil** by Suzanne Williams, illustrated by Steven Kellogg (1997). A librarian brings reading to a small town and to a television-watching gang, as well.

**The Library Lion** by Michelle Knudsen, illustrated by Kevin Hawkes (2006). "One day a lion comes to the library."

**Souperchicken** by Jane and Herm Auch (2003). Dedicated to reading teachers, this is a story of the first chicken to learn to read and how she saves her aunties from becoming chicken soup.

**Tomás and the Library Lady** by Pat Mora, illustrated by Raul Colon. A young migrant worker learns to love books with the help of a kind librarian. A true story.

**Wild About Books** by Judy Sierra, illustrated by Marc Brown (2004). Librarian Molly McGrew parked her bookmobile in the zoo by mistake. And, the animals decide to build their own Zoobrary.

**Willy and Hugh** by Anthony Brown (1991). A chimp who reads to his gorilla friend—the story of a friendship.

# *part two:*
# BOOK VENTURES

Although this collection of Great Books began in 1986 with choices made by participants in Minnesota Women's Press book groups who met at our offices in St. Paul, it was expanded in 1996 to include choices made by readers in the book groups conducted by Glenda Martin in Arizona.

The year 1996 also saw the beginning of two other ongoing book ventures—Retreats and Travels (Book Groups on the Road; Books Afoot, and "happenings.") Participants in all of these also selected a "great book."

Reading Retreats were created for those wishing a peaceful time away, immersed in books, surrounded by other book lovers. Reading four to six books around a theme, as well as reading poetry and children's books together, women gather for a two-or-three-day getaway for discussion, debate, laughter and sharing of stories. Retreats have been held in Minnesota, Arizona, Michigan, Washington, New Jersey and New Mexico.

Book Groups on the Road and Books Afoot were created for those who love a combination of travel, walking and reading. By 2007, groups have traveled to: Alaska; Boston and Amherst, Mass.; Carmel, Calif.; Colorado Rockies; Iceland; England's Lake District; London; Maine coast; Monhegan Island, Maine; New Mexico; New York City; New Zealand; Scotland; Scottish Highlands; the Outer Banks of North Carolina; Vancouver Island, B.C.; and Yorkshire, England.

Often books read were written by authors from the visited area, many of whom met with participants. Exploration of the landscape was invaluable in enriching the books read, while visits to local bookstores, libraries, and historic sites added to the readers' sense of place.

Following is a sample of the books, individual experiences, and photos from 21 years of book groups, retreats, and travel groups. It is from all these experiences that books included in "The Great Books" have been chosen.

# GROUPS

In 21 years of facilitating book groups, I always begin with the following: "We are not school. No one has to read the book, or be concerned if only part has been read—feel free to ask questions and perhaps you may decide to read the book. We do not gather for an academic, analytical critique of the author's intent, but rather to explore the meaning of the book for our individual selves."

I also emphasize that, while many of the books we discuss will bring forth personal experiences, "We are not therapy." And, "it is the responsibility of the group to be sure no one person dominates the discussion."

Every group session begins with a question that I pose to the group, sometimes related to content of the book, sometimes not. We go around the circle, not skipping anyone. This is to build a woman-centered, book-loving community, where each woman has a story to share, and each voice is heard.

Never, until the session is ending, do I respond to reactions of liking or disliking the book. Too often, starting with the question, "Did you like it?" sets a tone that limits discussion.

While facilitating book groups for 11 years in Minnesota and 10 in Arizona, the most intriguing task for me always has been choosing a theme. Selecting books related to the theme is challenging and full of excitement, but the greatest pleasure comes from the diverse reactions in book groups as participants discuss whether the books relate to the theme. Each discussion is a stretch! —**Glenda Martin**

# Arizona groups read around a theme

**Is This Novel Novel?** For six 2006 book groups, the theme was "Is This Novel Novel?" The foundation book referred to at each session was **13 Ways of Looking at the Novel** by Jane Smiley, in which she wrote:

> *"…novels can be sidelined—dismissed to the seraglio (harem), where they are read by women and children and have no effect on those in power. When that happens, our society will be brutalized and coarsened by people who speak rather like us and look rather like us but who have no way of understanding us or each other."*

Is This Novel Novel?

To explore this theme we read: **The Ice Queen**, Alice Hoffman; **We Need to Talk About Kevin**, Lionel Shriver; **The Painted Drum**, Louise Erdrich; **Heir to the Glimmering World**, Cynthia Ozick; **Season of the Snake**, Claire Davis; **Snake**, Kate Jennings; **On Beauty**, Zadie Smith; **The History of Love**, Nicole Krauss; **Snow Flower and the Secret Fan**, Lisa See; **The Space Between Us**, Thrity Umrigar; **Oh My Stars**, Lorna Landvik.

**The Republic of the Imagination.** For eight 2007 book groups, the theme was "The Republic of the Imagination," which comes from an essay by Azar Nafisi in the Washington Post, Dec. 5, 2004:

> *"In us there is a far greater impulse —a longing for the universal, a desire for a shared humanity. It is in that leap toward middle ground that we move toward what truly binds us: toward culture, toward stories, toward language. And it is here, in the republic of imagination, that we are most humane."*

The Republic of the Imagination

These are the books read and discussed for this theme : **Night Watch**, Sarah Waters; **Suite Française**, Irene Nemirovsky; **The Inheritance of Loss**, Kiran Desai; **Cellophane**, Marie Arana; **Water for Elephants**, Sara Gruen; **Half of a Yellow Sun**, Chimamanda Ngozi Adichie; **The Floor of the Sky**, Pamela Carter Joern; **A Million Nightingales**, Susan Straight; **Broken for You**, Stephanie Kallos; **Labyrinth**, Kate Mosse; **The Thirteenth Tale**, Diane Setterfield.

# Minnesota groups

When Glenda went off to establish a new bookdom in Arizona, she asked me to take over her Minnesota book groups for five years. Eleven years later I am still facilitating two of them.—Denise Scheibe

**Sunday Novels Group.** Book Groups tend to wax and wane, but Sunday Novels New in Paperback, begun in 1992, has remained a strong, consistent group of fine bookwomen. Three of the original participants still faithfully attend. Here are the books we read in 2006:

Sunday Novels

**Evidence of Things Unseen,** Marianne Wiggins; **Purple Hibiscus,** Chimamanda Ngozi Adichie; **March,** Geraldine Brooks; **On Beauty,** Zadie Smith; **The History of Love,** Nicole Krauss; **Gardenias,** Faith Sullivan; **Four Souls,** Louise Erdrich; **Case Histories,** Kate Atkinson; **Small Island,** Andrea Levy; **The Book of Salt,** Monique Truong; **Highwire Moon,** Susan Straight.

**There is a lot of laughter in groups as can be seen in the Sunday Novels group above.**

**Booker Group.** The Booker Group, begun in 1994, has reinvented itself several times. Our current name stems for our decision to only read prize-winning novels—until we began asking the question, "Who on earth chose this book to be a prize winner?" Since then, although we haven't changed the name, we now choose to read what we believe will be "good books," prize-winners or not. Here are the books we read in 2000, when we adopted our current title:

The Booker Group

**An Awfully Big Adventure**, Beryl Bainbridge; **A Crime in the Neighborhood,** Suzanne Berne; **Fugitive Pieces,** Ann Michaels; **The Beginning of Spring,**

Penelope Fitzgerald; **I Was Amelia Earhart,** Jane Mendelsohn; **Foreign Affairs,** Alison Lurie; **Paradise,** Toni Morrison; **A Spell of Winter,** Helen Dunmore; **The Bone People,** Keri Hulme; **The Essence of the Thing,** Madeline St. John; **Fasting, Feasting,** Anita Desai; **Interpreter of Maladies,** Jhumpa Lahiri.

**Sunday Together Group.** In 1990, the Sunday Together Book Group began at Minnesota Women's Press. It evolved out of several book groups which had been reading around Spirituality themes.

Every third Sunday morning of the month, 30-40 women gather in a circle, respond to a query from the facilitator and share an experience, before dividing into three book groups—Rock, Earth and Weavers.

Some of the women would say they have found a spiritual home in Sunday Together. Some would say they have found an intellectual home where there is the challenge of ideas. Some would say they have found a sense of place, of trust, of acceptance as they explore ideas not universally accepted. Some would say they have found meaningful friendships that have flourished over the years.

All would say Sunday Together is a community of women to which they are thankful to belong.—Glenda Martin

Sunday Together; Earth, Weavers and Rock

# RETREATS

Book groups create strong connections among those who love to read. Over 21 years, hundreds of book groups with thousands of participants have been facilitated through Minnesota Women's Press, Inc.

But if readers love a book group, what about an entire weekend away, totally immersed in what has been read, sharing reactions with others over breakfast, lunch, dinner, and even a glass of wine? How about adding a poetry walk, a film, children's books with messages for ages 3-93?

Thus began Reading Retreats, 58 of them as of 2007, held in Minnesota, Arizona, Michigan, New Mexico and New Jersey.

Following are the 30 themes used and the books discussed. Some participants thought a book read fit the theme and others did not. It's what makes for great discussion. The Great Books have a * beside them. For some retreats we've included films, children's books, and poetry used.

Here's a challenge. Pick a theme, read the books listed and write to us about how the books fit or did not for you. Or use it for your book group and relish the diversity as well as the tension of reactions. Makes for the best kind of discussion.

## 1996 Sense of Place

**Celebrating the Land: Women's Nature Wrting 1850-1991,** Karen Knowles; **Desert Quartet: An Erotic Landscape,** Terry Tempest Williams; **\*Gift from the Sea,** Anne Morrow Lindberg; **I Know Why the Caged Bird Sings,** Maya Angelou; **\*Journal of a Solitude,** Mary Sarton; **\*Lost in Translation: A Life in a New Language,** Eva Hoffman; **Rainy Lake,** Mary Rockcastle; **Rift,** Lisa Cody

## Mysterious Women

**\*Ancestral Truths,** Sara Maitland; **\*Ceremony,** Leslie Marmon Silko; **\*Housekeeping,** Marilynne Robinson; **\*Out of Time,** Paula Martinac; **Surfacing,** Margaret Atwood.

## Women in the Woods

**\*North Spirit: Sojourns Among the Creek and Ojibway**, Paulette Jiles,
**Smithson's Island: the Necessity of Solitude**, Judith Ann Smiths, **\*Solar
Storms**, Linda Hogan, **Two Old Women: An Alaska Legend of Betrayal,
Courage and Survival**, Velma Wallis, **\*Into the Forest**, Jean Hegland

## Food for Body and Soul

**\*Drinking the Rain: A Memoir**, Alix Kates Shulman; **\*Fried Green Tomatoes at
the Whistle Stop Café**, Fannie Flagg; **The Gastronomical Me: Essays**, M.F.K.
Fisher; **Hunger's Table: Women, Food and Politics: Poetry:** Margaret Randall

*Films:* "Like Water for Chocolate" based on Laura Esquival's novel and "Babette's
Feast" based on the story by Isak Dinesen.

*Children's book read aloud:* **Wildflower Tea** by Ethel Pococki

## Wise Woman

1998

**Charms for the Easy Life**, Kaye Gibbons; **\*Drinking the Rain: A Memoir**, Alix
Kates Shulman; **\*The Hundred Secret Senses**, Amy Tan; **Anything We Love
Can Be Saved: A Writer's Activism**, Alice Walker

## The Sensuous Self

1999

**Aphrodite: A Memoir of the Senses**, Isabel Allende; **\*Ex Libris: Confessions
of a Common Reader**, Anne Fadiman; **How Reading Changed My Life**, Anna
Quindlen; **The Mistress of Spices**, Chitra Banerjee Divakaruni; **Spending, A
Utopian Divertimento**, Mary Gordon

## Women of Adventure

**\*Annapurna: A Woman's Place**, Arlene Blum; **Two Old Women: An Alaska
Legend**, Velma Wallis; **Blind Descent**, Nevada Barr; **\*The Fires of Bride**, Ellen
Galford

## Intellectual Homelessness

2000

**\*Cactus Thorn: A Novella**, Mary Austin; **Janet Frame: An Autobiography**,
Janet Frame; **Paris Was A Woman: Portraits from the Left Bank**, Andrea
Weiss; **The Search for Signs of Intelligent Life in the Universe**, Jane Wagner;
**Wounds of Passion: A Writing Life**, bell hooks

*Film:* "Paris Was a Woman"

*Poetry:* Marge Piercy, Robin Morgan, Mary Oliver and Susan Griffin.

> Intellectual homelessness? What's that?
>
> Participants in the "Intellectual Homelessness" retreat in 2000 put forth some ideas.
>
> **1. What is intellectual homelessness?**
>
> "Definitions will be individual." "It can be both a limitation and a creative force." "One needs to experience homelessness to get to the next level of an intellectual home." "It is not a one-time, one-place thing." "An intellectual is always at home and always homeless."
>
> **2. What is an intellectual home?**
>
> "A community." "Solitude." "A place where we can own that we're smart." "Where asking questions is honored." "Where one has opportunity to live the questions." "In words, in the beauty of language." "When I connect with an author I'm reading." "When I read authors to find who I am." "When I get goose bumps."

## Beginnings

**Alma Rose**, Edith Forbes; **Kindred**, Octavia Butler; **Housekeeping**, Marilynne Robinson; **Stones for Ibarra**, Harriet Doerr.

*Film*: "Housekeeping"

## 2001 Best of Friends

**\*Hummingbird House**, Patricia Henley; **Old Books, Rare Friends: Two Literary Sleuths and Their Shared Passion**, Leona Rosteberg & Madeleine Stern; **\*The Robber Bride**, Margaret Atwood; **Seasons of Sun and Rain**, Marjorie Dorner; **\*Sula**, Toni Morrison

## Creating New Worlds

**\*Into the Forest**, Jean Hegland; **\*Gate to Women's Country**, Sheri Tepper; **Herland**, Charlotte Perkins Gilman

*Films*: "Bagdad Café" and "All I Wanna Do"

## 2002 Creative Reading: Brings You to a Different Place

**\*Breath and Shadows**, Ella Leffland; **\*Nine Parts of Desire**: **The Hidden World of Islam Women**, Geraldine Brooks; **\*The Handmaid's Tale**, Margaret Atwood; **Written on the Body**, Jeanette Winterson; **Love Invents Us**, Amy Bloom; **The Devil's Chimney**, Anne Landsman

## Books With a Bite

**\*Cactus Thorn: A Novella**, Mary Austin; **\*Driver's Seat**, Muriel Spark; **Lambs of God**, Marele Day; **The Prowler**, Kristijana Gunnars; **Snake**, Kate Jennings

## All History is Fiction, and Personal

**\*The Dress Lodger**, Sheri Holman; **Year of Wonders: A Novel of the Plague**, Geraldine Brooks; **\*Fugitive Pieces**, Anne Michaels; **\*Moon Tiger**, Penelope Lively; **\*A Chorus of Stones: The Private Life of War**, Susan Griffin; **Enemy Women**, Paulette Jiles; **In the River Sweet**, Patricia Henley

## Going Forward, Looking Back

**\*The Dollmaker**, Harriet Arnow; **All Passion Spent**, Vita Sackville-West; **Pavilion of Women,** Pearl S. Buck

*Film:* "The Dollmaker"

## Living on the Edge, Where?

**\*Holding the Line: Women in the Great Arizona Mine Strike of 1983**, Barbara Kingsolver;**\*Kissing the Virgin's Mouth**, Donna Gershten; **Lathe of Heaven**, Ursula K. Le Guin; **\*Waist High in the World: A Life Among the Nondisabled**, Nancy Mairs; **\*Woman Warrior: Memoirs of a Girlhood Among Ghosts**, Maxine Hong Kingston; **Woman Who Watches Over the World: A Native Memoir**, Linda Hogan

## Is Life All About Stuff?

**Lambs of God,** Marele Day; **My Year of Meats,** Ruth Ozeki; **Moral Hazard,** Kate Jennings; **\*Two Old Women,** Velma Wallis; **\*July's People,** Nadine Gordimer

Reading poetry aloud, at the "Is Life All About Stuff?" retreat, held at the Weber Center in Adrian, Mich. The setting is a cemetery—an appropriate venue for the theme, we thought.

## Do You Belong: Where, When, Why, With Whom?

**\*July's People**, Nadine Gordimer; **\*Two Old Women: An Alaska Legend of Betrayal, Courage and Survival**, Velma Wallis; **\*When the Emporer Was Divine**, Julie Otsuka; **\*The Book of Dead Birds**, Gayle Brandeis, **\*In the Name of Salome**, Julia Alvarez; **La Tzu Tao Te Ching: A Book About the Way and the Power of the Way, A New English Version**, Ursula K. Le Guin; **The Last Life**, Claire Messud; **Dwellings: A Spiritual History of the Living World**, Linda Hogan

*Film*: "The Station Agent"

## Beyond Familiar

**The Story of an African Farm**, Olive Schreiner; **Nervous Conditions**, Tsitsi Dangarembga; **Brick Lane**, Monica Ali; **The Namesake**, Jhumpa Lahiri
*Film*: "Monsoon Wedding"

## 2005 Where Believers Travel

**\*Death Comes for the Archbishop**, Willa Cather; **\*The Last Report on the Miracles at Little No Horse**, Louise Erdrich, **Books and Islands in Ojibwe Country**, Louise Erdrich; **Herland**, Charlotte Perkins Gilman; **Days of Plenty, Days of Want**, Patricia Preciado Martin; **Skywater**, Melinda Worth Popham; **Papago Woman**, Ruth M. Underhill

*Films*: "Ballad of the Sad Cafe" and "The Lathe of Heaven"

## A Numinous Happening: Becoming a Book/Literary Artist

**The Wave in the Mind: Talks and Essays on the Writer, the Reader, and the Imagination**, Ursula K. Le Guin; **\*What I Loved**, Siri Hustvedt; **Small Rocks Rising**, Susan Lang; **\*Evidence of Things Unseen**, Marianne Wiggins; **\*Breath and Shadows**, Ella Leffland; **\*A Chorus of Stones: The Private Life of War**, Susan Griffin

*Children's books*: **Before You Came This Way** and **Everybody Nees a Rock** by Byrd Baylor, and **Amadito and Spider Woman** by Lisa Bear Goldman

*Documentary:* "The Great Story" by ecotheologian Thomas Berry

*Poetry:* Mary Oliver, Linda Hogan, Emily Dickinson, Joy Harjo, Gail Tremblay.

## Women Authors' Books into Movies

**The Prime of Miss Jean Brodie**, Muriel Spark; **Mrs. Dalloway,** Virginia Woolf; **Chocolat**, Joanne Harris; **Rabbit-Proof Fence**, Doris Pilkington; **A Thousand Pieces of Gold**, Ruthanne Lum McCunn

*Children's book read aloud:* **Nurse Lugton's Curtain,** Virginia Woolf

## Is Love a Score of Zero?

**Annie John,** Jamaica Kincaid; **The Bluest Eye,** Toni Morrison; **\*The Center of Everything,** Laura Moriarity; **\*The Time Traveler's Wife,** Audrey Niffenegger; **\*What I Loved,** Siri Hustvedt; **\*Evidence of Things Unseen,** Marianne Wiggins; **Four Souls,** Louise Erdrich

> "The theme for the retreat "Is Love a Score of Zero?" was hashed and rehashed, but no definite decision was reached.
>
> It was generally agreed that love is a balance, a force for both good and evil, definitely a driving strength in all our endeavors.
>
> Two traditions of these retreats—the Saturday evening gathering for wine and an examination of children's books, and the Sunday "poetry walk" in the surrounding woods, seemed to strike a chord with all. Should not each of us have more poetry in our lives?"
> —**Maxine Dehn, Effingham, Ill.**

## Happily Ever After

**\*Breath and Shadows,** Ella Leffland; **The Idea of Perfection,** Kate Grenville; **Tales of a Female Nomad: Living at Large in the World,** Rita Golden Gelman

## Literature is the Path: Books, Libraries and Labyrinths

**2006**

**\*The Archivist,** Martha Cooley; **\*Evidence of Things Unseen,** Marianne Wiggins; **The Telling,** Ursula K. Le Guin; **High Tide in Tucson: Essays From Now or Never,** Barbara Kingsolver; **\*Ex Libris: Confessions of a Common Reader,** Anne Fadiman,

## Is Life a Mystery? Or Is It Fate?

**\*Book of Dead Birds**, Gayle Brandeis; **Holes,** Louis Sachar; **Miniatures,** Nora Labiner; **The Painted Drum,** Louise Erdrich

*Film:* "Holes"

### The Power of Words: Whose Reality Is It?

*Bee Season, Myla Goldberg; Heir to the Glimmering World, Cynthia Ozick; Miniatures, Norah Labiner; *Snow Flower and the Secret Fan, Lisa See; Ella Minnow Pea, Mark Dunn

### Deep Reading in Ancient Land

*Ceremony, Leslie Marmon Silko; Cactus Thorn, Mary Austin; Writing the Sacred into the Real, Alison Hawthorne Deming; *Red: Passion and Patience in the Desert, Terry Tempest Williams; *Yellow Woman and a Beauty of the Spirit, Leslie Marmon Silko; Songs of the Flute Player: Life in the Southwest, Sharman Apt Russell; Face to Face: Women Writers on Faith, Mysticism and Awakening, Linda Hogan and Brenda Peterson.

### The Way We Were?

The Canning Season, Polly Horvath, The Color of My Words, Lynn Joseph: I Hadn't Meant To Tell You This, Jacqueline Woodson; Out of the Dust, Karen Hesse

*Film*: "Fly Away Home"

## 2007  Living at a Border: Whose?

American Chica: Two Worlds, One Childhood, Marie Aran;,The House of the Scorpion, Nancy Farmer; *Highwire Moon, Susan Straight; Mother Tongue, Demetria Martinez; The Tale of Despereaux, Kate DiCamillo

*Children's books read aloud:* I'm in Charge of Celebration and Moon Song, each by Byrd Baylor

### The Truth of Fiction

Highwire Moon, Susan Straight; Making It Up, Penelope Lively; Moral Hazard, Kate Jennings; Suite Française, Irene Nemerovsky

### The Republic of the Imagination)

The Inheritance of Loss, Kiran Desai; *Cellophane, Marie Arana; Water for Elephants, Saara Gruen; *The Floor of the Sky, Pamela Carter Joern; The Book Thief, Marcus Zusak

*Film*: "Pan's Labyrinth"

How blest we are
while living in a time
of fear and violence,
to come to a place of such
peace and history,
to share it all,
the inner experience,
the beauty of the Earth,
with other kindred souls.

—Mary Lou James, participant

The pleasures of reading retreats—time spent with other reading women, talking books and exploring ideas, listening to each other and sharing stories— sometimes cause participants to break into poetry!

*Twelve motley women 'neath the great red rocks;*
*Eleven sit and listen while another one talks.*
*What are these women doing here?*
*Does anybody know?*
*Pulled from different places*
*By an inner undertow.*
*She holds a book in one hand,*
*A pen clasped in the other;*
*A sister joins a sister,*
*A daughter joins a mother.*
*Whose story lies inside this book?*
*What magic does it hold?*
*One book strikes a woman's soul,*
*Another is left cold.*
*Pain is no stranger to this group,*
*Each has known loss and grief;*

*They share it with each other;*
*They trust and feel relief.*
*The young one listens carefully;*
*She's started on her way;*
*The elders smile their blessings;*
*They know she'll be okay.*
*Different though these women are,*
*They have a common goal;*
*To find their peace in time and space,*
*Somewhere that feeds the soul.*
*The women listen and they speak,*
*They read and write and dream,*
*Of dragons and unicorns,*
*And other things unseen.*

Exploring the range of their own artist-selves, the readers of the "Numinous Happening" group (2005) created with words, images, clay and inspired interaction. Norma Shapera of Green Valley, Ariz., penned this poetic description of the group.

# TRAVELS

The idea of doing "book groups on the road" stemmed from the great interest our book group participants had in traveling to places they read about, and their curiosity about the home ground of particular authors. Along the way, we added places that we had simply always wanted to go to, without knowing what kind of writing by women we would find. In every instance, we were stunned by the wealth of reading available and the joy with which authors welcomed our interest.

Sometimes we've gone back to previously visited areas, but mainly we keep covering new ground, with still more places beckoning us.

These adventures are a way for us to see places we've never seen, or return to spots we've wanted to revisit. Reading the words of the women who lived there and wrote about what was in their hearts, as well as discussing them with like-minded souls, immeasurably enriches the experience and allows us to explore the landscapes that inspired the authors and the cultures that shaped them.

We meet with local writers and readers, hold book discussions each day, and visit local book shops and libraries. And, as in every good book group, we learn about ourselves in the process.

Following are some of the book-travel ventures we've facilitated. We've listed them alphabetically, by place.

# Alaska, May 2006

Although plenty of women are writing in and about Alaska—our three-pages-long list of books by Alaska women writers contained many fine memoirs, essay collections, historical accounts and poetry—we discovered that not many of them are writing fiction set there.

There seems to be something about the dramatic landscape that encourages the telling of, and reflecting on, true stories more than imagined tales.

"Alaska calls us to write nonfiction," said Nancy Lord, author of the acclaimed memoir **Fish Camp** and the book of hers that we all had read, **Green Alaska: Dreams from the Far Coast.**

"The place and stories are very dramatic here," she told us. Stories of people being eaten by bears, for example, or floating away on ice floes, walking hundreds of miles to safety in the middle of winter, living through months of darkness. "And Alaska draws a lot of odd people, who make great material for writers."

So in a time when "people are looking for authentic stories," Lord said, there hasn't been as much need in Alaska to turn to fiction.

—Excerpted from an article by Mollie Hoben in BookWomen, Aug.-Sept., 2006

Looking for just the right rock on Alaska's Fox Island, at 9 p.m. with the sun still high in the sky.

Alaska reading:

**The Alaska Reader,** Anne Hanley and Carolyn Kremers

**Flight of the Goose,** Lesley Thomas

**Green Alaska: Dreams from the Far Coast,** Nancy Lord

**Heart of the Sound,** Marybeth Holleman

**Two Old Women** and **Raising Ourselves,** both by Velma Wallis

# B oston & Amherst, June 2005

On a June New England afternoon, our small band of book lovers drove up to an old farmhouse in Lincoln, Mass., outside Boston. In the front yard, writer Elizabeth Graver awaited us, with one young daughter on her hip and the other shyly looking out from behind her legs.

We had come to talk with Graver about her novel, **Unravelling**. and talk we did. We told Graver about how her novel touched us; she told us about her writing life, the influence of children on her work, her approach to fiction.

"I never like anything that feels like a neatly tied-up ending," the writer said. "I'm interested in thorny people, characters who you can't say if they're doing the right thing or not."

The Boston area is rich with wonderful old libraries, and the group visited several.

Boston reading:
**Unravelling,**
Elizabeth Graver

**Murder at the Gardner,**
Jane Langton

**The Orchard**, Adele
Crockett Robertson

**Work,** Louisa May Alcott

**The Wedding,**
Dorothy West

Emily Dickinson poetry
and letters

She hopes her writing achieves what she herself seeks as a reader: "I read to enter another world, to be transformed. I don't read to be happy, but to understand."

Graver was one of six writers whose work we had read in preparation for our Book Group on the Road. By the time our week in Boston ended, we felt we came to know each of them in new ways, as we met them (directly or indirectly), experienced the landscapes that influenced them, and delved into their work in our discussions.

—Excerpted from an article by Mollie Hoben in BookWomen, Aug.-Sept., 2005

## Carmel, California, November 2005

Twenty women spent a week in Carmel, Calif., immersed in the life and work of writer Mary Austin; an independent woman who wrote fiercely, though never simply.

During a visit to the history library in Carmel, we became immersed

Carmel reading:
**The Ford,** Mary Austin

**A Woman of Genius,**
Mary Austin

**The Land of Little Rain,**
Mary Austin

**Cactus Thorn,**
Mary Austin

**I-Mary: A Biography of
Mary Austin,**
Augusta Fink

*Two essays by Austin:*
"Frustrate" and "Friend in
the Wood"

in some of Austin's original work, including one of her plays "Fire," based on a tribal legend of how fire was discovered. In 1913 the play was performed at the outdoor Forest Theater, so we journeyed there and played out our own performances on the stage.

A visit to the home Austin had built in 1906, including a "wick-i-up," a platform built in the branches of an oak tree where she went to write, filled us with awe.

**Sunset draws Carmel book group members.**

We walked the trails of Point Lobos, where Mary Austin picnicked with Jack London, George Sterling, and James Hooper, during the time of the early Carmelites.—Recollections by Glenda Martin, facilitator

## Colorado, May 2000

Colorado reading:
**A Lady's Life in the
Rocky Mountains,**
Isabella Bird,

**The Magnificent
Mountain Women,**
Janet Robertson,

**An Owl on Every Post,**
Sanora Babb,

**No Reck'ning Made,**
Joanne Greenberg

When 16 readers went to Estes Park, Colo., Beverly Todd, founder of the local Literature by Women book group, wrote about it in BookWomen, Aug.-Sept. 2000.

"Friday night the Book Group on the Road met with Trail Ridge Writers, a group of poets in Estes Park, to which I also belong. We gathered at the home of BookWomen subscriber Bea Williams, co-founder of the group, where we had the unforgettable experience of reading our poetry to women who listenened intently, smiled, asked questions, and then asked us to sign favorite poems that had been published in a small book by Minnesota Women's Press.

It was absolutely intoxicating to read to such a receptive group. Everyone in our poetry group loved every minute of it. It was a strong reminder that poetry is meant to be heard."

# Iceland, June, 2002

We were intrigued by Iceland because it is one of the most literate cultures in the world, boasting many talented women writers. But when we looked for books by Icelandic women published in English, we could find only three, so these were the books we asked the group to read. Yet despite this arbitrary selection of titles, we found that the three novels complemented each other well. And taken together, they gave us a rich introduction to Icelandic culture and women's lives.

Icelandic writers have always known they won't be translated widely, said Frida Sigurdardottir, one of the writers with whom we met. In the 1990s that began to change, but there's still not a lot of interest in most Icelandic literature. "In other countries they think we are very gloomy."

Icelanders have always traveled, Frida said, and they always return, bringing back new ideas and knowledge of the world. When we asked what draws them back to this small, isolated place, she replied, without hesitation, "The land." —Excerpted from an article by Mollie Hoben in BookWomen, Aug.-Sept., 2005

Iceland reading:
**Z—A Love Story** by Vigdis Grimsdottir
**The Prowler**, by Kristjana Gunnars
**Night Watch**, by Frida Sigurdardottir
**Laexdala Saga**, written about 1250

# London, September 2003

Zadie Smith (**White Teeth**) quietly appeared at the library in northwest London where we were gathered one evening, and she talked with us for about an hour, even though she was leaving in two days for a semester of lecturing at Harvard and was busy getting ready.

Sara Maitland came in to London from her home in rural County Durham to have lunch with us and show us around the area of London where her novel **Three Times Table** is set.

Mystery writer Susan Moody

**Zadie Smith signs copies of her novel for Books Afoot group fans.**

London reading:
**All Passion Spent**, Vita Sackville-West
**Heat of the Day**, Elizabeth Bowen
**Three Guineas**, Virginia Woolf
**Three Times Table**, Sara Maitland
**White Teeth**, Zadie Smith

invited us to her Oxford home, along with two writing pals of hers, who joined her in serving us a "proper English tea," while talking to us about their writing lives.

Can it get any better than this for a group of avid readers?

—Excerpted from an article by Mollie Hoben in BookWomen, Dec.-Jan., 2004

Maine reading (from four Maine book trips):

**Country of the Pointed Firs,** Sarah Orne Jewett

**House by the Sea,** May Sarton

**Island Garden,** Celia Thaxter

**As the Earth Turns,** Gladys Hasty Carroll

**High Tide at Noon,** Elisabeth Ogilvie

**Sailing,** Sally Kenney

**The Edge of the Sea,** Rachel Carson

**Spoonhandle,** Ruth Moore

**Drinking the Rain,** Alix Kates Shulman

**Wednesday's Child,** Rhea Cote Robbins

**The Weight of Water,** Anita Shreve

**Island in the Bay,** Dot Simpson

**Stern Men,** Elizabeth Gilbert

**Carrying Water as a Way of Life: A Homesteader's History,** Linda Tatelbaum

**My World Is an Island,** Elisabeth Ogilvie

**In the Country of the Young,** Lisa Cary

*Children's books read aloud: A Walk Through the Woods,* May Sarton, *A Penny for a Hundred,* Ethel Pochocki.

# Maine, May 1997, May 1998, June 1999, June 2001

Maine was selected as a travel reading group destination in 1997 because members of the May Sarton book group at Minnesota Women's Press had asked for years, "When are we going to York, Maine?" This is where Sarton lived for 22 years until her death in 1995. Though Sarton died before we got there, we visited York and stood outside her house by the sea. It would be the first of four Book Groups on the Road to Maine. Two more groups also explored the Maine coast, from Saco to Downeast, and one group spent a quiet summer week on Monhegan Island, where we not only talked about books but also tried our hands at drawing and painting.

"Being in the places and meeting or hearing about the authors made the writing come to life. To have the beauty of the land and sea, the architecture of homes, the quaintness of the towns, the sea spray, and

**The 1997 Maine travel group gathers around the statue of Edna St. Vincent Millay in Camden.**

even the weather—sun and clouds—all real for my eyes to see was special."—**Emmy Lou Jacobson**, participant, 1997

"Our Sunday morning at the Rachel Carson Wildlife Refuge was an incredible spiritual experience: the power of building our bookwomen community using words from **The Edge of the Sea** and **Always, Rachel** for our liturgy, set in the glory of the cathedral of tamarack, maples and salt marsh. The image of the scarlet tanager moving through the preserve with us is one of my heart's treasures."—**Kathleen Keating**, participant, 1997

# New Mexico, November 1996, 1998 & 1999 (Ghost Ranch)

When 15 women set out for New Mexico on the first Book Group on the Road, I wondered—would this work? Our goal was to hold book discussions each evening and to immerse ourselves each day in the land we had read about. This plan worked so well another 19 women went to New Mexico in 1998, and another group the following year.

Touring Georgia O'Keeffe's house in Abiquiu, I had a vibrant mind-picture of her looking out at her views and walking through the garden.

At the San Ildefonso pueblo of potter Maria Martinez, about whom Alice Marriott wrote, we walked the plaza where Maria and her husband Julian had lived. We stopped in shops where Maria's descendents sell pottery based on what they learned from Maria.

Just up the road from the pueblo we viewed the remains of Edith Warner's small house where she entertained the scientists from Los Alamos more than 50 years ago, captured in the story by Peggy Pond Church.

**Readers in the New Mexico group explore the stunning landscape at Ghost Ranch.**

We found it doesn't take long to become acquainted with book-reading women. Friendships are made quickly and laughter fills the day.

After our days exploring, we gathered for book discussions back at Ghost Ranch. We learned that reading authors from a given area, then traveling there, greatly enhances discussion and brings us in touch with the author. Finally, we learned that each of us contributed to making such a journey what it becomes—magic.

—Excerpted from an article by **Barbara Clark** in BookWomen, Aug.-Sept., 2005

# New Mexico, November 2004 (Pojoaque)

"Having read more than 25 of her books I feel as if I have known Sheri Tepper for 15 years. From her writing I was expecting a strong woman with strong opinions and a highly developed sense of humor. She was all of that and more.

New Mexico reading, from three trips (at Ghost Ranch):

**Maria, the Potter of San Ildefonso,** Alice Marriott

**House at Otowi Bridge,** Peggy Pond Church

**Mother Tongue,** Demetria Martinez

**Ceremony** and **Storyteller,** Leslie Marmon Silko

**Southwestern Women: New Voices,** Caitlin Gannon

**Portrait of an Artist: A Biography of Georgia O'Keeffe,** Laurie Lisle

**Death Comes for the Archbishop,** Willa Cather

**Face of an Angel,** Denise Chavez

**Walking to the Edge: Essays of Resistance,** and **Hunger's Table: Women, Food and Politics,** Margaret Randall

**Miss O'Keeffe,** Christine Taylor Patten

**Intimate Landscapes: the Canyon Suite of Georgia O'Keeffe,** Dana Self

**Two Lives: A Conversation in Paintings and Photographs:** Georgia O'Keeffe & Alfred Stieglitz

**Canyon of Remembering,** Lesley Poling-Kempes

**What This Awl Means: Feminist Archaeology at a Wahpeton Dakota Village,** Janet D. Spector

New Mexico reading
(at Pojoaque):

**The Family Tree** and
**The Fresco,**
Sheri Tepper

**All Over Creation,**
Ruth Ozeki

**Dwellings: A Spiritual
History of the Living
World,** Linda Hogan

**Lao Tzu Tao Te Ching:
A Book About the Way
and the Power of the
Way,** a new English
version by
Ursula K. Le Guin

**Wild Life,** Molly Gloss

She owns the 34-acre guest ranch, Rancho Jacona, were we stayed. She shared with us her early love of the natural world. Our theme, 'Ortho-ecology,' is a term coined by Tepper. The world's ecology is meant to be self-sustaining, but humanity has broken many crucial components in the balance. By prefacing ecology with 'ortho' she evokes the medical meaning of 'correcting maladjustments.' Literally, to straighten out what has been broken.

Writer Sheri Tepper leads the New Mexico book group on a tour of the edenic environment she's creating at Rancho Jacona, in Pojoaque.

As she took us on a tour of the ranch, it was evident that Tepper loves her land and takes pleasure nurturing it. She is a great role model. She started her life over at age 50 when she began her career as an author. Twenty years later, looking at all she has accomplished, I wonder what I could get done by 2025?"

—Excerpted from an article by **Lou Ambrose**, participant, in BookWomen, Aug.-Sept., 2005

"I savored the peace of the ranch with domestic animals grazing and peaceful Pojoaque River views.

A special treat was meeting the astonomer Peter Lipscomb. We took turns gazing upward through his telescope as he related myths and stories about the constellations. Another highlight was meeting in Santa Fe with a 30-year book group from Albuquerque to talk about **All Over Creation** by Ruth Ozeki over wine and supper.

Sheri Tepper joined us to talk about **Family Tree** as well of the history of Rancho Jacona. The land was first inhabited by native people and then came under Spanish rule. The ancient irrigation system, called acequias, is still used today. The ranch is Tepper's attempt to carve out a simpler, sustainable way of life and live in a community with the people who keep it going.

The best part of every book retreat is getting to know the women in the group. By the end, I always feel I have made many new friends. The retreats have become necessary to feed my creative spirit and my sense of adventure."—Excerpted from an article by **Pauline Loewenhardt**, particpant, in Book-Women, Aug.-Sept., 2005

# New York City, June 2007

Memories of a book week...

... Standing at the site of New York City's horrific Triangle Shirtwaist fire of 1911 while Katharine Weber read a moving account from her novel **Triangle** of that fateful day....

... Sitting in the inviting, book-lined living room of Amy Koppelman's Upper West Side apartment overlooking the Hudson River and talking with an upbeat Amy about her life and her dark novel **A Mouthful of Air.**

... Meeting with Katherine Lanpher to hear the author of **Leap Days** tell what she's been doing since her midlife move from Minneapolis to the Big Apple.

... Stopping to commune with the impressive new statue of Eleanor Roosevelt by sculptor Penelope Jencks.

... Relishing the incredible opportunity to meet Paule Marshall, writer of the classic **Brown Girl, Brownstones**, in her elegant pied-a-terre in the West Village.

**Katharine Weber reads from her novel "Triangle" at the site of the tragic fire.**

... Mingling with the colorful crowd at the Broadway musical, "The Color Purple."

... Visiting Hue-Man Books in Harlem, the nation's largest African American bookstore.

... Cruising the marble corridors of the New York Public Library on a guided tour that included a look into the gated stacks.

—Excerpted from an article by participant **Cathy Anderson** in BookWomen, Aug.-Sept., 2005

New York reading:

**Brown Girl, Brownstones,**
Paule Marshall

**Leap Days,**
Katherine Lanpher

**A Mouthful of Air,**
Amy Koppelman

**Triangle,**
Katharine Weber

**Wild Nights: Nature Returns to the City,**
Anne Mathews

**Woman Unafraid; Where the Action Was;** and **Girls: A History of Growing Up Female in America,** Penny Colman

# New Zealand, October 2001

We went to New Zealand because it sounded like a wonderful thing to do, and whenever the subject came up it seemed everyone else thought so too—so we went, and it was glorious!

During our 16 days there, we traveled in planes, trains, passenger vans, buses, ferries, tramcar, cable car—and many of us in a yacht built for the America's Cup in 1996—and we covered as much of both islands as time allowed.

We lived in home stays, B&Bs, motels, a convent, a college and a castle.

We met renowned New Zealand authors who seemed as awed by the fact that we had read their work and traveled such a distance to meet

Three of New Zealand's most respected writers—Patricia Grace, Barbara Anderson, and Fiona Kidman—met with the group to talk about their work, and to laugh a lot, as well.

New Zealand reading:

**The Bone People,**
Keri Hulme

**The Book of Secrets,**
Fiona Kidman

**Potiki,** Patricia Grace

**Long Hot Summer,**
Barbara Anderson

**The Silicon Tongue,**
Beryl Fletcher

**Cowrie,** Cathie Dunsford

**In a Fishbone Church,**
Catherine Chidgey

**Janet Frame: An
Autobiography**

**New Zealand Stories,**
Katherine Mansfield

**The Story of a New
Zealand River,**
Jane Manders

them as we were to meet them. All commented on our courageousness at making the trip in light of the Sept. 11 happenings. They were welcoming, sincere, and had terrific senses of humor.—Excerpted from an article by Denise Scheibe, in BookWomen, Dec. 2001-Jan. 2002

"The women I have met on this journey—both co-readers/travelers and authors—are as amazing as the landscape of New Zealand. Our universal connection with each other has been (and is) words. The conversations have been equally diverse, interesting, provocative, surprising, warm and funny. It's been a great experience.—**Mary Ann Cordova**, participant

"Spectacular beauty. This experience has been one of a community of readers, the intellectual exchange of interpretation and definition. Meeting authors enhances not only their writings, but New Zealand and Maori culture."—**Pat Rustad**, participant

"Before the recent arrival of settlers, much of New Zealand was covered in native forests. Today there are only remnants of the forests left, but they give a glimpse of the millions of years this earth belonged to the plants.—**Wanda Newsted**, participant

"On our hike to the Franz Joseph glacier, we followed a dry stream bed toward the mass of ice. Rounding a corner in the trail we were confronted with a trio of waterfalls. Some places on earth are so beautiful they take your breath and halt your feet."—**Judy Young**, participant

"Reading the books first and then going on the trip is like traveling there twice.—**Terri Foley**, participant

Combining miles and books is a great way to travel. Our literary map not only took us to several high points of New Zealand but to significant places we had read about in the books, bringing the stories to another level. Meeting the authors will be a memory to treasure for a lifetime."—**Kay Humphreys**, participant

## Scotland & Yorkshire, August 1998, August 1999

In 1998 we ventured outside the United States for the first time, traveling to Scotland and Yorkshire with an eager group of 15 reading women. In preparation, we had read 11 books by women from the region. A number were authors unknown to the readers until then, but all became favorites!

Being in the incredible landscapes that formed the backdrops for the books—the North Sea, the purple moors, the austere Highlands, the ancient fishing villages, the cities where castles and cathedrals fill the skylines—enriched our reading and nourished our spirits. And we were drawn back to the area the following year for two more adventures.—Mollie Hoben, co-facilitator with Denise Scheibe

"The interweaving of the landscapes and characters in the books we read with the people and places our travels revealed was uncanny and incredible."—**Rosalie Wahl**, participant

"Now my reading has a real background of scenery—'place'—that adds so much. As we walked in York and Whitby we were moving where characters we read about had walked. Great!"—**Emmy Lou Jacobson**, participant

"How exciting and satisfying: to see the moors where Heathcliff and Cathy walked (**Wuthering Heights**); to go to the very places Christabel and Ash explored (**Possession**); to see the "heather on the hill" that I've always read about; to tour the Highlands, with the sun, then the rain, then the fog, the mountains and the rivers, the rainbows."—**Virg Ledo**, participant

"The books we read really made the trip come alive. Now I'm going to reread them, and I know I will enjoy them again. Meeting with the Whitby book group was special, as was meeting with the authors."—**Lois Harms**, participant

"Seeing the physical settings of the books gave me a better appreciation of the authors' perspectives and the forces that shaped them."—**Barbara Blackstone**, participant

"People who read and love to travel are compatible and have much to talk about in formal and informal discussions. The lovely scenery let us know the settings of our reading. The climate, too, let us know where some traits of character might come from!"—**Betty Ann Burch**, participant

Scotland reading:

**O Caledonia,** Elspeth Barker

**Keeping up with Magda** and **Giving Up on Ordinary,** Isla Dewar

**Fires of Bride,** Ellen Galford

**Finding Peggy** and **Holy City,** Meg Henderson

**Gowk Storm,** Nancy Morrison

**The Prime of Miss Jean Brodie,** Muriel Spark

**Ancestral Truths,** Sara Maitland

Yorkshire reading:

**Behind the Scenes at the Museum,** Kate Atkinson

**Wuthering Heights,** Emily Bronte

**Possession,** A.S. Byatt

**Crusoe's Daughter,** Jane Gardem

**Apothecary Rose,** Candace Robb

**Jane Eyre,** Charlotte Bronte

**Flither Pickers,** Theresa Tomlinson

Occasionally groups get a little rowdy , but if you have Rosalie Wahl with you, she'll keep them in line! At Stirling Station, Scotland, her walking stick turned into a handy tool.

Whitby Book Group met with us at Sneaton Castle in Whitby, N. Yorkshire.

# Taos, November, 2002

Participants in two Book Groups on the Road stayed on the grounds of the Mabel Dodge Luhan house, now a retreat center. Luhan lived in Taos from 1918 until her death in 1962.

Taos reading:

**Mabel Dodge Luhan: New Woman, New Worlds,** Lois Rudnick

**Winter in Taos,** Mabel Dodge Luhan

**Death Comes for the Archbishop,** Willa Cather

**Cactus Thorn,** Mary Austin

**Top of My Lungs** and **Writing Down the Bones,** Natalie Goldberg

We ate sumptuous meals in her dining room, walked the cemetery where she is buried, held discussions in the log cabin she built for her son, and read aloud to her in her bedroom from her memoir **Winter in Taos**; legend has it that when Mabel is present one can smell cinnamon, and some of the women were sure they could.

The group in Mabel Luhan's bedroom listen to the reading from her memoir, as the smell of cinnamon wafts through the air!

—Glenda Martin, co-facilitator with Denise Scheibe

"After talking together over a gourmet dinner and concluding an introductory session we felt a transition beginning. Surprisingly soon, we became one solid book group, eager to know more about each other and the magic and mystery of the Southwest." I would prescribe a Book Group on the Road with an array of good books and a convergence of wonderful women. That is really all you need to get high and stay smiling for weeks thereafter and perhaps forever."—**Larae Essman**, participant

# Vancouver Island, B.C., August 2004

Although the books we read were quite diverse, we found that several themes threaded themselves through all our reading.

Vancouver Island reading:

**Burial Ground,** Pauline Holdstock

**Cure for Death by Lightning,** Gail Anderson-Dargatz

**Daughters of Copper Woman,** Anne Cameron

**Klee Wyck,** Emily Carr

**Monkey Beach,** Eden Robinson

**Obasan,** Joy Kogawa

The most striking theme—reflecting our experience in the forest—was the creative and spiritual power of the natural world. In every book we read, the landscape was a key part of the story: a connection to history, a source of awe, a companion, the home of spirits and mysteries. Another theme we encountered in our reading was the meeting of the different cultures of B.C.—First Nations, European and Asian—which has led to tragic clashes, domination and discrimination, but also enrichment.—Excerpted from an article by Mollie Hoben, in BookWomen, Oct.-Nov., 2004